The
Triune God
of
Christian Faith

Zacchaeus Studies: Theology

General Editor: Monika Hellwig

The
Triune God
of
Christian Faith

by

Mary Ann Fatula, O.P.

A Michael Glazier Book
THE LITURGICAL PRESS
Collegeville, Minnesota

A Michael Glazier Book published by The Liturgical Press

Cover design by David Manahan, O.S.B. Chi-Rho symbol, mosaic detail, 5th century baptistry of Albenga, Italy.

	4	5	6	7	8	9

Library of Congress Cataloging-in-Publication Data

Fatula, Mary Ann.
    The triune God of Christian faith / by Mary Ann Fatula.
      p.   cm. — (Zacchaeus studies. Theology)
    "A Michael Glazier book."
    Includes bibliographical references and index.
    ISBN 0-8146-5765-6
    1. Trinity. 2. Trinity—History of doctrines. 3. Catholic
Church—Doctrines. I. Title.   II. Series.
BT111.2.F38 1990
231'.044—dc20
                                                 90-62040
                                                   CIP

Contents

Editor's Note

This series of short texts in doctrinal subjects is designed to offer introductory volumes accessible to any educated reader. Dealing with the central topics of Christian faith, the authors have set out to explain the theological interpretation of these topics in a Catholic context without assuming a professional theological training on the part of the reader.

We who have worked on the series hope that these books will serve well in college theology classes where they can be used either as a series or as individual introductory presentations leading to a deeper exploration of a particular topic. We also hope that these books will be widely used and useful in adult study circles, continuing education and RENEW programs, and will be picked up by casual browsers in bookstores. We want to serve the needs of any who are trying to understand more thoroughly the meaning of the Catholic faith and its relevance to the changing circumstances of our times.

Each author has endeavored to present the biblical foundation, the traditional development, the official church position and the contemporary theological discussion of the doctrine or topic in hand. Controversial questions are discussed within the context of the established teaching and the accepted theological interpretation.

We undertook the series in response to increasing interest among educated Catholics in issues arising in the contemporary church, doctrines that raise new questions in a contemporary setting, and teachings that now call for wider and deeper appreciation. To such people we offer these volumes, hoping that reading them may be a satisfying and heartening experience.

Monika K. Hellwig
Series Editor

Introduction

This book on *the Triune God of Christian Faith* appears at
the end of the Zaccheus theology series not because Christian
faith in the Triune God is an addendum to our experience and
belief but because it is its very center, the culmination toward
which all the other dimensions of our faith converge. Yet
although the triune God is the heart of our faith, we Christians
often do not know it. One of my students said to me recently,
"The Trinity seems to be the best-kept secret in modern Christian history." Indeed, it is difficult to find the "Trinity" or
"triune God" listed in the subject index of many contemporary
theology books.

The reasons for this profound deficiency are many and
varied. First and foremost, the very depths of the mystery itself
incline us to silence. But it is also true that life-giving preaching
about the Trinity flows from actual experience of this God
transforming our lives in the midst of a loving community.
Perhaps many of us today, preachers and hearers of the Word
alike, have little personal knowledge of this conversion of life
and commitment to community that was so central in the
early church. In addition, we find it particularly difficult to
speak about the Trinity today because of major shifts occurring
in christology and the doctrine of God—shifts due to the
impact of re-interpretations of Chalcedon and feminist critiques of male symbols and language about the Trinity. Under
these problematic circumstances, it is often easier to say nothing about the Trinity; thus ignorance about this most central
reality of our faith continues. My teaching experience over the
past twenty years, however, has convinced me that the triune
God is the magnificent banquet on whom our minds and

hearts were made to feast, and a little taste makes even the most initially uninterested person hunger for more.

In this small volume I attempt to make a first step toward answering this need. The limitations of space have required me to be selective about which dimensions of past and contemporary trinitarian theology I would present. Among the many approaches possible to this central mystery of our faith, therefore, I have tried to offer in these few pages the insights and synthesis which have been most meaningful to me and which have proved most illuminating to my students. My hope is to open readers to the meaning of the triune God for our concrete human lives, and in giving a taste of the vast riches of this God, to make the reader hunger for more. In this endeavor I pray that the Holy Spirit may be the interior teacher drawing the mind and heart of each reader to the treasures at the heart of God.

Of course, it is ultimately sheer folly to attempt to speak about the Trinity, simply because this unfathomable God, infinite creator of the vast mysteries of the universe, so exceeds all that our small minds could even begin to grasp. Yet great trinitarian theologians and mystics like Augustine, the Cappadocians, Aquinas, and Catherine of Siena also knew by experience that we must at least *try* to speak of the unspeakable, of the intimacy of this God with us, of the infinite vulnerability of a God who would disclose in trust and love for us the very secret of the divine life. Our speaking of the Trinity in this way is all the more needed today because so many of us think of the triune God as an abstract theory, transcendent in an absolutely distant and unapproachable way. In this book, therefore, I have chosen to focus on the triune God unveiled in our concrete history, in the paschal event of Jesus' life, death, resurrection, ascension and pentecost, and on the unbounded nearness and closeness of this God to us.

In addition, my teaching experience has convinced me that Karl Rahner was correct: the danger for us western Christians in general is not really tritheism—having such a clear sense of the distinction in God that we in fact believe in three gods— but rather, modalism, having little or no sense of the personal distinction in God.[1] Many of us think of God as one infinite "person" or force whom we simply address with three different names. For us, in fact, there is often no real distinction between the one we name Father, and Jesus or the Holy Spirit. While guarding the infinite unity of the one God, my own approach, therefore, attempts to illumine the mystery of the unique identity of each divine person. And although, as we shall see, the word "person" is problematic, even with its inadequacy, it is still the word which for us most meaningfully conveys the truth that the triune God is not "it" but supremely "thou," "you."

In the context of these emphases on the triune God intimately and distinctly unveiled and given to us in our concrete history, I attempt ultimately to illumine the meaning of the triune God for our human lives in a world needing the transformation that the trinitarian vision and values of interpersonal gift-love and mutuality alone can bring. We thus begin in chapter one by considering in an introductory way the above-mentioned central themes. And because for so many of us the Trinity is an abstract theory rather than the living God we actually *experience* intimately and powerfully present in our own lives, we consider at the start how our faith in the triune God is grounded not in dry theories but in human experience (chapter one): in an unsurpassed way in the paschal mystery—in Jesus' life, death, resurrection, ascension, and pentecost (chapter two), and then in the Christian community's experience and faith-articulation of this paschal event (chapter three). Finally, because so few of us could identify the Trinity as having any real impact upon or relevance for us and for the pressing problems which confront us on a world-wide scale, we consider how we are meant by our very sacramental initiation to experience this triune God intimately present in our own lives (chapter four), and to live out the radical implications of our trinitarian faith in how we relate to one another, especially to the poorest and weakest among us (chapter five).

I express my profound gratitude to my parents, Michael Nicholas and Rity Hyzy Fatula, for continually showing me in their own lives what it means to live the selfless gift-love at the heart of the triune God. I want also to thank my Dominican community, family, and friends for their faithful prayer and support; Sisters Mary Michael Spangler and Francis Gabriel Mahoney, Angelica Armstrong and Patricia Twohill; John

Fatula, and Ennio and Rita Fatula Mastroianni for their very helpful suggestions; the faculty development committee of Ohio Dominican College for their moral and financial assistance; my students for teaching me how truly alluring the triune God is; and my own esteemed teacher, William J. Hill, O.P., professor emeritus at The Catholic University of America, for selflessly sharing his extraordinary wisdom and clarity with countless grateful students, among whom I am blessed to count myself. Finally, with so many other readers and writers, I owe special gratitude to Michael Glazier, whose largesse of soul surpasses even the breadth and depth of his publishing contributions.

I pray that this small volume will help readers to know and savor by experience the meaning of Catherine of Siena's words: "You, eternal Trinity, are ... insatiable, you in whose depth the soul is sated yet remains always hungry for you, thirsty for you ... You ... are a deep sea: The more I enter you, the more I discover, and the more I discover, the more I seek you."[2]

1

The Triune God and
Human Meaning

"Your face, Lord, I seek. Hide not your face from me" (Ps 27:8-9). This cry of the psalmist speaks in some way the hidden yet inescapable thirst of each one of us to know the source and goal of our being. Who is this abyss of love whom we seek and desire, often without realizing it, and what is the meaning of this God for our lives as human persons? In this first chapter we consider in a preliminary way the key themes of this book in response to this central question. Our reflections begin by focusing first of all on how our faith in the triune God is grounded not in abstract speculation but in human experience: in the paschal mystery—Jesus' life, death, resurrection, ascension, and pentecost—and in the Christian community's experience and faith-articulation of this paschal event. Second, because so few of us seem to realize the central significance of the Trinity for our human lives, we reflect also on how the triune God is the origin, the goal, and the content of our human meaning precisely because we are created by and for an infinite gift-love. The gratuitous love which alone can satisfy our human thirst is nothing less than the very self of a God who is not the poverty of a solitary monad but the unbounded richness of interpersonal communion. Finally, our reflections focus briefly on one contemporary implication of our trinitarian faith as it calls us to mutuality in our attempts to articulate and live the trinitarian mystery in our lives.

A. EXPERIENCE OF THE TRIUNE GOD AS THE HEART OF CHRISTIAN FAITH

We begin our reflections by considering how our belief in the triune God is the very heart of our Christian faith, rooted not in dry theories but in the deepest dimensions of our human experience. As human persons, each of us is a living thirst for meaning, for love, for wholeness. And although we may try to escape the question, life itself sooner or later forces it to our consciousness: is there an answer to our ache for love and meaning? Christians confess Jesus as risen Lord of the universe, and in this, their central proclamation, they utter a glad and resounding *yes* to the above question: *yes,* there is wholeness for our personal brokenness, and *yes,* there is love that is healing enough for the wounds and thirst of the entire world.

But the Jesus which Christian faith confesses does not offer simply himself as the answer to our human existence. The Christian scriptures proclaim a risen Lord inseparable from the one who sent him, the one he knew intimately and tenderly as "Abba," "dear Father." And they proclaim a risen Lord given to us for one reason, to pour out among us through his life, death, and resurrection the healing love and communion of the Holy Spirit. Thus the ultimate paradox of Christianity: precisely because Jesus *is* its very center, Christian faith is not simply nor even finally about Jesus alone but about the triune God Jesus discloses to us as our source, our meaning, and the extravagant, definitive answer to all of our human longings.

At first hearing this statement may surprise us. Although we do confess faith in the triune God, many of us would not identify this God as the living God we actually experience in our own lives. We may know that our initiation into the Christian life is a baptism into the Trinity, that our sacraments are trinitarian celebrations, and that our entire creed is structured around a confession of faith in the triune God. And we may realize that our name, "Christian," is trinitarian, describing Jesus as the one whom the Father anoints (*christos*) with the Spirit so that the Spirit may anoint our own lives. Certainly, we are not unaware of how often we begin our prayer "in the name of" and end with "glory to" "the Father, the Son, and the Holy Spirit."

Yes, we do confess faith in a triune God; but to put the question bluntly, so what? Isn't the Trinity an unnecessary complication, an interesting but dispensable addendum to our faith, an abstract idea in technical books written for theological experts? What possible relevance can faith in a triune God have for our real life and for the urgent problems of our world, for crime and poverty, for unjust economic and political structures, for marginalization and oppression and the threat of nuclear war? Just as long as there *is* a God, what possible difference can it make to us and to the world whether this God is triune or not? This central question provides the focus for this book, and in this first chapter I would like to introduce the question by considering the three experiential sources which ground our faith in a triune God today.

1. The Foundational Christian Experience of the Triune God in the Paschal Mystery of Jesus

We need to recognize first of all that our Christian faith in a triune God did not come to us as a result of logical deductions about an esoteric, abstract truth. On the contrary, our faith in a triune God is rooted in our concrete human history; first of all, in the paschal event—the human experience of Jesus in his life, death, resurrection, ascension, and pentecost; second, upon the Christian community's actual experience of the triune God in the past; and finally, upon our own experience in the present. Our faith today, therefore, is not a matter of mere intellectual assent to the Trinity as if we were accepting the answer to a complicated math problem without understanding how the problem really works: "Yes, I believe that two plus two equals four, but in God's case, one equals three."

Rather, our faith in the Trinity is primarily a matter of a living relationship of trust with a God actually experienced as healing and loving us in a triune way. This is the living God unveiled and given to us in the radical events which are the life, death, and resurrection of Jesus; a God, therefore, who is given to us in our own *concrete human history*. The triune God comes to us not as mere words recited in a creed but as the living God of our lives, a God whose power can transform us today as surely as it transformed the early Christians.

2. The Christian Community's Experience and Articulation of the Paschal Mystery

This brings us to a second important consideration. Our existence in history is always mediated experience; living in the present means that we cannot escape being the benefactors of a heritage given to us by the past. Our own experience of the triune God's presence and activity in our lives today is inextricably linked with the foundational experience of the first Christians, with the apostles' and disciples' witness to the healing and liberating power of the risen Lord and his Spirit in their own lives and communities. Our faith in the triune God is thus a life-giving, future-oriented convergence of our own experience with that of the first Christians whose experience founds our own.

Yet our Christian faith is not simply a matter of experience but also of articulating the source and content of this transforming experience. We celebrate as a community the presence and power of the triune God in our midst, but we also communicate and hold out to others the possibility of making this same transformation their own. And so we human beings confess our faith in *words* which in our most fundamental proclamations come to us from the articulations of the early Christian communities. Among these proclamations, some hold special place because of their authoritative nature, for example, the articulation of the Council of Nicaea that Jesus is truly divine. But the doctrines to which we say *yes* are always themselves halting attempts to put into words what absolutely transcends all human thoughts and words, the ineffable God whose healing love we can actually *experience* in our lives.

The apostles and disciples spoke of what they actually had experienced in their own lives. Thus, the love which had radically changed them impelled them to preach, drawing others to open themselves to the risen Lord and the healing power of his Spirit. In turn, their love and proclamation inspired in still others a conversion which turned their lives literally upside down. Here was a whole new way to live, not enslaved and bitter and alone, but as persons in relationship, growing in freedom and love in the midst of a community who cherished them as equals. Here, in the family of the risen Lord, made new by the power of his Spirit, they came to know their own identity as daughters and sons of the one Jesus called "Abba." This most tender Father was also mother to them, a God whose love overturned all human patterns of domination and manipulation. Here in this community of the risen Lord they finally belonged as equals, bound together in relationships of mutuality and reciprocity. Here they learned to love in a way that in turn healed and freed others.

Their celebration of baptism, anointing, and the eucharist initiated them into the Christian community, into a new family and new way of living. After months and even years of preparation which focused on preaching, conversion and self-giving love in community, they celebrated their initiation into the Christian way in words which confessed the source, content and power of their new life. Thus, long before they were able to articulate clearly the triune identity of the God they experienced as transforming them, they spontaneously named this God in a tri-fold way: "I baptize you in the name of the Father, and of the Son, and of the Holy Spirit." That is, "I plunge your whole being into the depths of God, Father, Son, and Spirit. I immerse you, I drown you in God's infinite love which you experience concretely in this community and which you in turn will learn to extend to others."

Through their baptism they were plunged not simply into water, not simply even into a community of brothers and sisters, but most radically into the community of the living God, into the rivers of mercy at the heart of the triune God they experienced as making their own lives new. And through experiencing the community's love, they gradually began to recognize God as active in their own lives in inseparable and yet distinct ways.

Their savior Jesus had sacrificed his own life for them and now they knew his own tender "Abba" as their own. They also experienced the power of Jesus' Spirit as the very bond of their own communion with God and one another, making their lives a new creation. In contrast to so many times when they had resisted their own healing, when in fear and self-protection they had uttered an inner *no* in response to the offer of love, they experienced now a living *yes* within themselves to the freedom and wholeness offered them in the risen Lord. This inner *yes* drew them with such strength and freedom that it could be only the Spirit of Jesus binding them together. The radiance and warmth of this *yes* of love was so powerful within and among them that they could only cry out to the Spirit of Jesus, *Thou, You,* as to the living God and not merely as to an impersonal force.

In summary, for the early Christians, faith was a living relationship of love with the triune God and with one another, inseparable from the preaching, conversion, and community central to their lives. They were led to communion with the triune God through the preaching they continually heard, a preaching full of power because they could see this God at work in the lives of the preachers. And they experienced the strength of the triune God's love in an utterly concrete way through the commitment and love of their brothers and sisters in community. Through their membership in this community, their entire lives were turned upside down in a conversion that radically changed the way they had previously related to God, to themselves, to others, and to the world. For these Christians, the triune God was not an abstract and dispensable addendum to their lives but its very content.

3. Reclaiming Christian Experience of the Triune God Today

This last point leads us to a third important consideration. Most of us realize that although key words about the triune God remain in our Christian talk and prayer, they are often empty of any significant content for us today. We have language about a triune God in our liturgy and prayer, but often very little experience of the transforming power of the sacraments of initiation and of the Christian life in community which originally gave rise to these words.

This situation is not simply a recent phenomenon. After the fourth century, baptism sometimes became an advantageous way to promote economic, social, and political unity among tribes immigrating into Europe. At the conversion of their leader to Christianity, a whole people could be baptized *en masse,* with little or no instruction or catechumenate period. Gradually emptied of their original content and meaning, divorced from the preaching and conversion, and community that were central to the community's conversion experience in the early Church, the words of baptism not infrequently became just that, only words.

Even into our time, preaching and teaching on the Trinity either are passed over in silence or often resemble the discussion of a complex, theoretical math problem with little relevance for real life. We preachers and teachers ourselves perhaps have had little first-hand knowledge of the kind of personal conversion in community that formed the heart of the early Christian experience. Thus, sermons on more "practical" topics easily replace preaching about a Trinity viewed not as the living God but as an abstract theory beyond our understanding. The Trinity often becomes not only in theology books, but also in the ordinary Christian's head and heart, little more than a complex, unnecessary addendum to the supposed real task of Christianity, trying to lead a good, moral life through our own arduous efforts.

Yet because the primal experience of the early Christians founds our own trinitarian belief, we need to claim for ourselves, in our own world today, the transforming *power* and freedom which their confession of faith in a triune God attempted to articulate. To be Christian today thus means reflective and critical fidelity to the essential elements of our Christian heritage in scripture and tradition, yet in a way that enables us to respond to the ever new presence of the triune God active in our own experience and world.

B. THE TRIUNE GOD: UNBOUNDED GIFT-LOVE AT THE HEART OF OUR HUMAN MEANING

1. The Tri-Personal God: Interpersonal Gift-Love

We need to ask, therefore, what real difference it makes for our lives today that the living God is triune. In order to respond to this key question, we reflect here in a preliminary way on what it means to confess faith in a God who is not a unitarian monad, nor three gods, but tri-personal. We must say at the start that no human word or idea—limited as it is in its very nature—can grasp or contain the unspeakable transcendence of the triune God; all of our paltry ideas and words are infinitely more unlike than like who God is.

As we will see later, the modern conception of person, in particular, has connotations which we must immediately deny of the living God. The infinitely rich God who is not created matter but spirit, life, be-ing, goodness itself, is also not person in the created, limited way we human beings are persons, by being circumscribed by material bodies, or by being individual centers of consciousness. In addition, the word "person" does not have the same exact meaning even when applied to the three who are God, as if they are simply "clones," three exact instances of the same reality. Jesus himself is person by being also fully human, and the one he calls Abba, as well as the Spirit, are infinitely unique in the vast mystery of their own personhood. Thus, even the word "person" must immediately be denied of God, and then said again with the realization that God utterly transcends this feeble human word and the poverty of its content. The infinite God is truly *trans-personal,* that is, infinitely beyond all that our human experience identifies as "person."[1] Yet we use the word "person" of God not because it is adequate to describe God, but because, even with all of its limitations, it is still the most meaningful word we have to describe the most precious reality we know. We call God tri-*personal* because God is supremely *I,* infinitely *You,* not *It.*

One key advantage of the contemporary understanding of "person" is precisely its focus on relationship; as Martin Buber and other contemporary thinkers have stressed, to be person is to be in relationship.[2] There is, however, an infinite difference between us as persons and God as tri-personal. We are persons who *have* relationships with others. Our relationships are not *who* we are; they are not our sheer identity. But as Aquinas and contemporary authors such as Walter Kasper have empha-sized, the Father, Son, and Holy Spirit, who are infinite full-ness of life, do not *have* relationships with one another; they *are* their sheer relationship of love to one another. There is no divine person who is first or independently an "I" and then who is *also* Abba, "You," for Jesus. The entire personal identity of this Abba is an infinite relationship of love to Jesus in his humanity. The Father does not *have* but *is* eternally a living relationship of love to this Word who now reigns also in his humanity as risen Lord.

This way of speaking about the triune God as three distinct persons may seem at first hearing to be tritheism, belief in three separate gods. But we need only read the accounts of the Gospel of John and the Acts of the Apostles to see the reality of a God truly *experienced* by the early Christian communities— even if not yet able to be clearly articulated as such—as inseparably one and the same God and yet supremely distinct in a threefold way. In the experience of these early communities, Jesus is not his Abba, nor is this Abba the Spirit poured out among them with saving power through the death and resurrection of their Lord and Savior.

2. The Triune God and Our Human Meaning as a Thirst for Gift-Love

What are the implications for us that God is triune by being living relationships of love? Here we consider how we can live our Christian call to reach out in interpersonal love and care for the poor and oppressed only when we ourselves as persons are fed and nurtured by an infinite gift-love. Contemporary writers such as Karl Rahner stress that our very make-up as human persons consists in our identity as a living thirst for inexhaustible love and meaning.[3] I have been struck by these simple words of Dorothy Day, whose passion for peace and social justice might have led us to expect from her a more complex response to the world's ills: "What else do we want, each one of us, except to love and be loved?.... Even the most ardent revolutionist . . . is trying to make a world where it is easier for people to love."[4]

Yet what is love? Like Dorothy Day's response, the profound insight of Martin Buber strikes us with its simplicity: love is the relationship I—You. We love when we relate to another not as "It" but as "You": "Love is the responsibility of an I for a You."[5] A human existence closed in on itself, isolated and cut off from other persons, cannot survive. As babies we spontaneously reach out to clutch at anything. But anything is not enough. The urge and need to be *toward someone* else, to be in relationship, is our inmost necessity; without love we literally cannot live. Our aimless grasp for anything is in reality a grasp for someone.

A mother bends over the crib and smiles at her child . . . and one day, her child smiles back at her. A father gently fingers his baby's unbelievably tiny hand . . . and one day his baby curls these tiny fingers around those of the father's. At moments like these we glimpse what it means to be a human person. To be person is to be *I*, not *It*, and we become *I* only through relation to a *You.* To be someone—not something— is to be a living thirst for love, for relationship.

Christians see this most fundamental fact of our human identity in a light that is radiantly illuminated by Jesus' paschal mystery and by the triune God of love revealed in this event. We cannot live without love because we come from the hands of a God whose own personal being is the fullness of love's communion. The God from whose heart and womb we have come is not God as one in the poverty of an isolated individual, nor as a monad enthroned in a far away heaven, needing us in order to have someone to love. The God revealed in Jesus' death and resurrection is the ecstasy and communion of love at the very depths of the divine heart and being. It is in the image and likeness of this triune God that we are made and in whose infinitely free and lavish love we find the source and reason for our existence.

And here is the crux of the matter. A unipersonal God needs us in order to love. But the God who is triune communion of love does not *need* us in order to have someone to love. And for this reason, we are, each of us, *really,* unconditionally and freely loved. This statement may surprise us, for we easily identify need with love; to need someone is to love him or her, and to be needed is to be loved. Yet love is ultimately a matter not of need but of free gift, or it is not fully love at all.

We can love with what Abraham Maslow calls self-centered need-love or with an other-centered being-love. We love with need-love as children, but if we never grow beyond this kind of love as adults, the "loved" one is not truly a *You,* loved for his or her own sake and good, but is always an *It* for us, existing to fulfill our needs. Only relationship with a *You,* however, is enough to foster our growth as a mature *I.* When we love with gift-love we are drawn by the inherent beauty and goodness of another. We reach out of our own narrow, self-centered world to foster the good of one we love not as an extension of ourselves but as a unique and precious other, as *You.*

Maslow's and Buber's insights echo the distinction Aristotle and Aquinas make between self-centered love and mature, "friendship" love. In self-centered "need-love" we treat another as a means to our own happiness and goals. Yet this kind of love never truly enriches us because we do not reach out of the boundaries of our own narrow ego to the real being and richness of another. When we love with "friendship-love," however, we cherish another person as an equal and as "other." In this kind of mature love, we foster and work for our loved one's good as if it truly were our own. And, paradoxically, when we love with unselfish love we ourselves are enriched and expanded as mature persons, because our love unites us not simply to our own needs but to the reality and richness of the one we love. Obviously, loving with this kind of gift-love is not possible to our efforts alone; it requires a life-time of cooperation with God's grace healing and transforming our hearts. Yet this kind of loving is the goal toward which we are meant to grow until our hearts expand enough to take all the world's oppressed into their embrace.

This inescapable need finally to be loved and to love freely, as gift and graciousness rather than out of need, is the place in our own lives where we can discover the inestimable difference the love of the triune God does and can make for us. To be a human person is to be a living thirst for relationship, a thirst inseparable from who we are. Yet the ultimate thirst of each one of us is to love and to be loved freely, not out of need or expediency, but out of sheer gift, out of an unconditional choice and graciousness which truly cherish us in our own unique preciousness.

The reason for our thirst is that we have come from the hands of the God who is triune, who does not need us in order to love, who as tri-personal God *is* the infinite richness of relationship and givenness. We hunger for love as gift because we *are* loved as undeserved gift. Since we have been loved into being with infinite gift-love, the only fulfillment that will satisfy all of our longings is precisely this same infinite gift-love from whose womb we have received our entire being.

And if we seek the answer to our thirst, we need not cry out,

"O God, where can I go to find your face?" The mystery of the triune God is not high above us in the heavens nor merely outside of us, but also and most deeply in our midst, within us, present in the very make-up of our being. Because we are a thirst for unconditional gift-love, we are, to the core of our being, a trinitarian mystery. And so to talk about the mystery of the triune God is to talk also about our own mystery as human persons. In the triune God, we find our *own* identity and meaning, our *own* origin and goal.

The depths of the mystery we plumb in the Trinity, therefore, is God's mystery and at the same time inextricably ours. We are a living thirst for the very gift-love that in fact enfolds and permeates every inch of our being and every second of our existence. Yet we need consciously to claim this love for ourselves and to open ourselves actually to *experience* its power to transform our own lives. It is then that we can so give of this love that its power will heal others, and—we may dare to hope—the entire world.

C. SOME IMPLICATIONS OF OUR TRINITARIAN FAITH TODAY

1. The Source and Meaning of Jesus' Name for God, Abba

We will consider in greater detail in chapter five the radical implications of our trinitarian faith precisely for our Christian call to bring this healing and transformation to the world. At this point, however, we need to reflect on some implications of our trinitarian faith for the kind of language we use of the triune God. In particular, I want to articulate the perspective from which my own use of trinitarian language in the succeeding chapters emerges, so that the words of this book may not prove a hindrance to entering more fully into the mystery of the triune God.

The contemporary movement to foster relationships of equality and mutuality among women and men invites us to ask whether we can both treasure the gift of Jesus to us and the heritage of our tradition in the naming of God as Father, Son, and Holy Spirit, and yet also re-claim from our tradition images for the triune God that draw upon the richness of women's experience as well as that of men. In this way our human language about the triune God can serve both to deepen our relationship with the living God and also to foster the kind of mutual respect for one another that faith in this triune God demands of us.

We know that our cherished names for the divine persons stem from the early Christians' celebration of baptism as they plunged their lives into the transforming love of "the Father, the Son, and the Holy Spirit." These names in turn stem in a profound way from Jesus himself within his Jewish context, as he invited his disciples to enter into his own intimacy with the God he called "Abba." Scholars such as Jeremias and Schillebeeckx have shown that Jesus' experience of God as "Abba" was so central to his personal meaning that it claimed and defined his entire identity.[6] And while the Hebrew scriptures do sometimes speak of God acting toward us like a gentle mother (Is 49:14-15) or a tender father (Ps 103:13; Hos 11:1-4), biblical scholars also point out that the sacred Hebrew word "Yahweh" signified a God so transcendent that no devout Jew would dare even to pronounce this name. All the more, then, no Jew would have dared to address God with the startling intimacy which springs spontaneously from the lips of Jesus. The creator of the universe who dwells "in inaccessible light" and whose name no one can speak, Jesus dares to call "Abba."

The nearest and yet still inadequate approximation we have to this tender and close name are the words "Papa," "Daddy," "Dearest Father." Yet what is even more startling is that Jesus' experience of radical intimacy with this God, unheard of and even blasphemous within the context of the Jewish tradition, formed the heart of his own identity as unique Son of this Father.

And in an amazing act of love Jesus gives to his disciples a gift so radical that its use will distinguish them as his own. This most intimate and personal name which Jesus alone used of God is now to be the one by which they themselves are to commune with God as familiarly as children snuggle close to their mother's breast or lie safe and secure in their father's arms. Jesus invites his followers into such unreserved union with himself that his own experience of Abba's extraordinary closeness and care is to become our own: "When you pray, say, 'Father'" (Lk 11:2). And as we do so, the Holy Spirit prays within us: "When we cry, 'Abba! Father!' it is the Spirit himself bearing witness with our spirits that we are children of God" (Rom 8:15-16).

And so we, like the early Christians, treasure this first name by which we are baptized into the triune God of love. Yet even as we use the word "Father" of God, we also immediately have to deny it, and then reaffirm it on a level of utter mystery, for its meaning in reference to God infinitely transcends what we ordinarily mean by "father." For us, "father" is inseparable from male gender. But "God the Father" is not a man, any more than God is a cat or dog, for both maleness and femaleness, while rich in their own unique content, are created, absolutely limited ways of existing. The God who is life and goodness and be-ing itself infinitely surpasses and transcends all that it means to exist in the limited mode of being male or female.

2. The Abba Who Frees Us From Patterns of Domination and Calls us to Mutuality

Thus, even to say the cherished name "Father" is to refer to the infinite God with a human word that connotes by its very nature only a created, limited way of being. Undoubtedly, our own personal experience defines what the name "father" comes to mean to us. For some of us, the name "father" evokes a sense of gladness and faithful presence, of unconditional love and unselfish giving, of memories that make us smile with gratitude. But for others of us, the very word cuts into our hearts and opens wounds of abandonment and betrayal, of absence and abuse and pain we would give anything not to have known. Even with all of its beauty, Jesus' cherished name for God not infrequently has been used to promote the very antithesis of Jesus' own way of relating to others, especially women.

The Gospels, in fact, show Jesus relating to women in a way radically different from what we would have expected of him in the context of his own culture. Jesus shocks the apostles by engaging in public conversation with a woman, even a despised Samaritan, and he treats her with respect as an equal (Jn 4:7-30). He praises Mary for sitting at his feet and drinking in God's word in a way that had been reserved only to men (Lk 10:38-42). After the resurrection he shows himself first of all to the women (Mk 16:1-11; Mt 28:1-10; Lk 24:1-11) and appoints Mary Magdalen as "apostle" of the resurrection's good news to the men (Jn 20:1-18).

Even Jesus' use of the name "Father" reflects a God who, far from fostering patriarchal power, calls us through Jesus into a totally new kind of family. Here, love and mutual respect are to reign, simply because it is with this kind of love that we are loved by God. The one Jesus calls "Abba" knows and cares for each one of us so intimately that every single hair on our head is counted (Mt 10:30). This Abba refuses to give up on us, searches for us when we sin, and covers us with kisses in our very weakness (Lk 15:18-23). This is the God who desires to be trusted without reserve and yearns to lavish infinite care on each one of us in our every need (Mt 7:11; Lk 11:13).

The extreme intimacy with which Jesus speaks of "Abba" portrays this God as both mothering and fathering us. Yet the transcendent God of Jesus is neither man nor woman nor any other created reality, for all human words stand dumb before the absolute mystery of God. In referring to the most precious reality we know, reality that is personal, reality that is *You*, not *It*, our human language offers us only the choice between male and female images, nouns, and pronouns. The images and words available to Jesus to address the God he experienced as radically close and intimate thus were inevitably drawn from his own Jewish background. On one level, Jesus' choice of the tender name "Abba" for God reflects the context of his own culture, for the Hebrews opposed the depreciation of women fostered by the surrounding nature religions in their worship of a mother goddess. While seeming to exalt woman to the status of the divine, such religions in fact reduced her value to the fertility of her body.

The God of Jesus, in contrast, calls us to a conversion from relating in prideful and domineering ways. This is the God who draws us together in a community of the risen Lord

where women and men are to respect, cherish, and relate to
one another as equals. Jesus' use of the name "Abba" for God,
far from fostering the subjugation of women to men, stands in
fact as a radical critique of patriarchal systems: "Do not call
anyone on earth your father. Only one is your father, the one
in heaven" (Mt 23:9). Thus, the God of Jesus defines the
meaning of all true fatherhood and motherhood, and not the
other way around; indeed, Jesus himself, in his own person,
radically re-defines the very meaning of the word *God* for us.
In using the name "Abba" for God, Jesus thus robs of its
absolute power every institution or pattern of relating which
would compete with the supremacy of the God of love and
mutual service. At the same time, he aims a searing critique
precisely at the patriarchy from whose power he intends to
free his disciples, and calls us to an entirely new kind of family
based not on the ties of kinship and fate but upon grace and
freedom.[7]

Jesus thus takes a word of tender familiarity, a word little
children used of their very own fathers, and, applying it to the
God who utterly surpasses the limitations of male gender,
gives it a radically transcendent meaning. The name "Abba"
for Jesus thus does not mean "man" nor any other created
reality. What, then, does it mean? Here is the heart of the
matter: when we say "Father" of God, we speak of a mystery
which absolutely exceeds anything in our own present experience, a mystery whose depths will be uncovered to us only in
the joy of heaven. While we wait, we use the name "Father"
for the first divine person not because it is an adequate word,
but because it is an approximation of Jesus' own intimate
name for God. It is, therefore, the name which bespeaks his
own intimacy and equality with his Abba and his own identity
as beloved divine Word and Son. Thus it is also the name the
early Christians prayed as they entered into Jesus' death and
resurrection through their baptism. As Jesus' disciples, we are
called to recover for ourselves the depth content of his name
for God, and to open ourselves to the extraordinary strength
and tenderness of this God in our own lives. At the same time,
Jesus' use of the symbol "Abba" for God calls us to create by
our love a different way to be together, a world in which
women and men respect and relate to one another as equals in
the family of the triune God.[8]

3. The Triune God as Source and Challenge for Our Relating in Mutuality

It follows from what we have said that our halting words in speaking of the triune God are truest when they foster this kind of equality and mutual respect and love among us.[9] This is one reason why we are recapturing aspects of the Christian tradition which refer to the triune God with images drawn also from women's experience.[10] Our baptismal naming of God as Father, Son, and Holy Spirit certainly remains normative for us. But we also know that no name is able to express adequately the infinite fountain of life, unity, beauty, and goodness that is the triune God. Thus, as we re-claim our central Christian heritage of actually experiencing the triune God at work in our lives, we are also inescapably called to deeper respect for one another in our ability to image the triune God's love in our own uniqueness as women and men.

Here I find the suggestion of Patricia Wilson-Kastner helpful. "Inclusiveness in language about God does not mean that each word or phrase about the trinitarian God must be sex-neutral or have male and female (or exclusively female) terms side by side." Rather, inclusiveness means a fidelity to our baptismal heritage in naming God as Father, Son, and Holy Spirit, and a simultaneous openness to other images from our tradition.[11] Thus, Julian of Norwich writes of the nurturing love of Jesus our Mother, while Catherine of Siena envisions the Holy Spirit feeding us with love at the breast of God.[12] At the same time, we need also to discover anew and live the truth, beauty, and depth-meaning of the symbol and name "Abba" which Jesus has given us.

The God from whose womb of love each one of us has been born is a tri-personal God in whom there is no relationship of domination or manipulation. Our faith in this triune God requires us to live out the implications of our trinitarian origin and goal in the mutuality of our respect, love, and service to one another. Our trinitarian faith calls us to allow the triune God of interpersonal love to become increasingly transparent in us, in the way we relate to one another and especially to the most vulnerable and wounded among us and throughout the world. Then will our faith in the triune God become the mystery of love in which we more and more consciously "live and move and have our being." The Trinity will be the living presence in and among us of the God whose love heals and transforms not only us, but also through us, the entire world.

2

The Paschal Event of Jesus and the Triune God of our History

We have reflected on the significance of the triune God for us in our human meaning as a thirst for gratuitous love. At the same time, we have seen how our trinitarian faith is grounded in the experience of Jesus and, derivatively, in the community's experience and our own today. We turn now to reflect in detail on the unsurpassable event of history which grounds our trinitarian faith, the paschal mystery—Jesus' passing over to new unbounded life through his life, death, resurrection, ascension, and pentecost. As we consider the meaning of these events, we begin to understand more deeply how the triune God reveals in them the infinite gift-love which alone fulfills our thirst as human persons.

The unveiling of the Trinity in the world's history and in our personal history as well is not a proposition about an abstract, eternal truth utterly divorced from our human experience. On the contrary, far from being a detached deity coldly existing beyond all time and space, unrelated to us and the vicissitudes of our lives, the triune God whom Jesus unveils to us is the living God whose love has involved itself irrevocably with us in our human history. The significance of the triune God for our own human lives thus raises a key question which we consider now in this chapter: how did our faith in the Trinity begin; how did we Christians come to experience a God who is triune? This question about the source of our belief in a triune God transcending the limitations of human history takes us paradoxically to a concrete occurrence in history so radical that it has changed the meaning of all history.

A. THE TRIUNE GOD AND HUMAN HISTORY

At the very center of our faith in the triune God, we confess a world-shattering event: in Jesus, God has entered into the stuff of our human lives, into the times and places and events that make up our day-to-day existence. Love itself has bound itself irreversibly to our concrete life for better and for worse, in a union more powerful than even death itself. The one we confess as God the Word and Son has entered into all that makes up our humanness; he has lived our life and died our death of misery. In Jesus, the triune God of heaven and earth has taken our history as God's own. In this way, an unimaginable mystery has closed our human meaning: through the incarnation of the Word, God has become our family. And because of this, even more, through grace we have become God's own family. In Jesus our human life with its joy and pain, with its fear and death, has become God's own; in Jesus, our history has become God's own history.

But Jesus has lived his human life and death in an unsurpassable way, as a saving pasch, a "passing over" through love to a whole new kind of human existence, from one who in his humanness *has* life to one who *gives* life, to one who has become in his risen humanity life-giving Lord and healing Savior of the universe. In Jesus, life itself now reigns over both our life and our death; a whole new kind of life and an unspeakably different kind of death are possible for us because of him. Paradoxically, we thus come to know the triune God of love who transcends history only by entering into a radical event of history, by entering into the depth of Jesus' humanity and history and seeing there the unrestrained love of the triune God unveiled in his human face.

In this chapter, therefore, we approach the mystery of Jesus not yet "from above," from the perspective of his divinity, but first of all, "from below," from the perspective of his humanity. And we ask the meaning for us of his human experience, of his life, death, and resurrection, and what the saving event of his pasch lived in our concrete history has to do with the triune God who befriends us with infinitely gracious gift-love.[1]

B. THE GROWTH OF JESUS IN HIS HUMAN CONSCIOUSNESS

Luke tells us that Jesus truly grew in wisdom, age and grace (Lk 2:52). But how did this maturing take place? We know that we come to our own self-consciousness, our own self-recognition and self-definition, in communion with others and what they reflect to us about ourselves. We read a passage that deeply moves us, we hear a word that touches us to the core of our being, and we cry out wordlessly within ourselves, "This describes *my* experience; in this word I recognize *myself.*"

At home in the arms of Mary his mother, at the knee of Joseph, at prayer with them at home and in the synagogue, Jesus drinks in the scriptures they love. As he listens to these scriptures and as he hears Mary and Joseph pray, surely a spontaneous cry of closeness with the God about whom he learns begins to well up within the heart of Jesus. This is the God so transcendent that the divine name "Yahweh" could not be pronounced. Yet Jesus begins to know and address this God by a name of shocking, even blasphemous intimacy and familiarity: "Abba," "Dearest Father."

He begins to hear the scriptures proclaimed in a way no one else did or possibly could; in growing to recognize the absolutely transcendent God of heaven and earth as his own "Abba," Jesus comes to know in an increasingly conscious way his own identity as unique Son of this "Abba." As he hears the description of the suffering servant in Isaiah 53, and the proclamation of Isaiah 61, "The Spirit of the Lord is upon me...", as he listens to these and myriads of other passages, surely Jesus begins to find himself described in them.

In other ways, too, he begins to recognize consciously his own identity. As a youth Jesus works beside Joseph, learning from his loving and skilled hands the carpenter's trade. But early in his adult life he hears about another man who also evokes his respect and admiration. One named John is proclaiming the imminence of an event awaited by the prophets and holy people of Israel, the coming of God's kingdom. John is baptizing those willing to enter wholeheartedly into the repentance that will make them ready for this reign.

Like attracts like. We spontaneously recognize the heart and soul of one given over to God when an immense and infinite desire for that same God fills our own being. Jesus is drawn to this young man in whom he feels so deeply God's presence; he is drawn to hear his words, to enter into his circle, and to receive his baptism. But what did John's baptism mean? The *anawim,* the lowly, humble Jews who put their entire trust in God, had longed for the kingdom of God to overtake Israel and so to establish the peace and justice of the endtime itself. Led by God's Spirit, John preaches the radical nearness of this final reign of God and invites anyone who will listen to enter symbolically into the floodtide of this kingdom.

John's preaching poses for his hearers a radical challenge to conversion and a way to ritualize their conversion: "Do you want to be part of God's reign on the brink of breaking through into the world? If you want to enter into the flood tide of God's mercy, do it physically. Let your entire person be plunged into this water and let this action symbolize the surrender of yourself to the infinite mercy of God's reign in your heart and midst." In company with the crowds and yet mysteriously separate from them, Jesus experiences a profound *yes* welling up from his heart. And so he presents himself to John for baptism. " *Yes,"* he cries out by his action, "Yes, let the full reign of God come upon me. Let God reign completely in my body and soul, in my mind and heart and whole being." And the prayer he was used to saying in company with his Jewish brothers and sisters in the synagogue becomes in a mysterious way fused with the identity of his entire being: "may your kingdom come upon me and upon all of us."

Recently a student said to me, "When I was ten years old, I had a sense that God wanted me to be a doctor. I don't mean a doctor to make money. I mean that this is *who I am."* Whether or not we could have clearly articulated its significance at the time, many of us also can think of a crucial, perhaps unobtrusive, turning point which has even unconsciously directed the course of our life from that moment on. The evangelists see in Jesus' baptism a profound experience of his being claimed by the Father, of knowing himself as the Father's beloved Son, of handing over his entire life to the reign of this God whom he knows intimately as Abba. Jesus claims his own identity and mission in absolute self-giving to his Father and dedicates himself to bringing about God's reign among his people.

But another turning point in Jesus' personal journey happens: like the prophets before him, John the Baptist is killed. Shaken by the implications of this death, Jesus goes apart to pray. He struggles with the meaning that John's death has for his own life and mission. He emerges from this time with his Abba knowing that he himself must proclaim not only the imminence of God's reign as John had done, but its very presence: "The reign of God is *here,* in your very midst." But the unutterable truth which no one could guess is that the reign of God is present because Jesus himself is present. Jesus not only brings the kingdom of God; Jesus *is* the kingdom of God in person. In him, God completely reigns. Jesus holds back nothing of himself for himself; everything he is, everything in him, is not only a radical gift from his Abba but also a total and unreserved gift back to his Abba.

C. A LIFE OF UNCONDITIONAL LOVE

Jesus begins proclaiming the kingdom of God at hand. As he does so, the compassion and mercy of his heart reach out and touch people. The Gospel accounts give us a sense of the tremendous magnetism of Jesus' person. He has to retreat to deserted places because people will not leave him alone. Parents with their sick children; tax collectors and prostitutes and all kinds of sinners; the crippled and the maimed; lepers and outcasts from the community; all seek him out.

As Jesus proclaims the kingdom of God at hand, his heart is touched with compassion and mercy for the people who come to him. And his mercy is effective; miracles happen. We have all had experiences of grieving over a loved one and being willing to do anything in the world to bring him or her to peace and health again. How often we have longed to change a situation, to reverse a tragic outcome, to turn back the course of death for someone we love, but have found ourselves powerless to do so. Yet when Jesus reaches out to someone suffering, his love does not simply long for healing the way ours does; his love gives healing. Jesus yearns over people and the flood tide of his compassion breaks forth from his heart not simply as deep feeling but as love that truly heals and transforms.

And even if he himself does not say it in words, he acts not only as one who ushers in the presence of God but who also *is* himself the presence of the God who loves with absolutely unreserved gift-love. At a time when no respectable Jew would speak in public with a woman, Jesus not only converses with women but also treats them as equals. Luke tells us of Mary sitting at his feet and drinking in his word as only men had been considered worthy of doing (Lk 10:38-41). John recounts a story of Jesus' profound conversation at the well with a half-breed and despised Samaritan woman, a woman who then evangelizes others (Jn 4:7-26). John tells also of Jesus' first resurrection encounter with the converted Mary Magdalen and his sending her as the first "apostle" of the good news (Jn 20:11-18). Jesus' compassion drives him to communion with every possible outcast. Eating with others is an act of communion with them, and Jesus' communion is with sinners; he pursues the ones no one else will love or touch. Jesus' company is with the tax collectors, with the publicans and outcasts, with those who have no place at the Hebrew table, with those who belong to no one.

But Jesus not only accepts sinners who come to him, he goes and seeks them out. This point Luke makes clear in his poignant story about the prodigal father (Lk 15:11-32), a parable about one who lavishes his love on the child who breaks his heart. While the son is off squandering his inheritance in selfish and reckless abandon, the father waits at home praying against all hope for his son's return. A series of misfortunes makes the young man finally come to his senses; while he is still far down the road that leads home, his father catches sight of him. He runs to meet his child, throws his arms around his neck and joyfully brings him home to a gala party celebrating his return; the dead child has come back to life, the lost one has been found! We are, each one of us, this lost child. And Jesus can tell this parable of the Father's lavish and tender compassion for us only because this is the kind of love that fills his own heart.

Unlike other rabbis whose disciples sought *them* out, Jesus himself chooses his own. But his choice is not just of the rich and powerful but also of the castoffs as well. Jesus seeks out every single one, especially the poor, the least regarded, the people no one else wants. And Jesus' disciples are not to stay in his company simply for a training period and then move on. No, they are asked to surrender irrevocably to him everything they have and are. Surely this is one of the key points of the parable about the widow who gives her last penny to the temple treasury after others give huge amounts they will never miss. They have plenty more left at home. But with Jesus, it is not the million dollars that we actually give that matters. It is the little penny we hold back in our other hand, just in case, as security for a rainy day. The discipleship Jesus asks of his own is not just a big piece of themselves, but everything.

This kind of radical claim on people's lives provokes from the chief priests and pharisees an antipathy that eventually will result in Jesus' death. He himself begins to see that the same fate that befell the prophets, that befell John the Baptist before him, will surely happen to him. Like others who slowly grow to see that the transcendent purpose of their lives will be accomplished only through the paradox of their deaths, Jesus begins to understand that the reign of God will come not only through his life but also through handing over his entire being to his Abba in death.

D. THE PASCHAL MYSTERY: THE LAST SUPPER AND CRUCIFIXION

1. The Last Supper

Those of us who have been with loved ones at death know that at these last moments dying persons are not capable of anything except yielding themselves over to the forces of death. At this time when all life force is being drained from them, when every energy must be spent simply in the tortuous task of gasping for the next breath, dying persons cannot speak the meaning of their life, nor of their death. If the unfinished business has not been attended to before this moment, if the words of reconciliation and good-by have not been said already, there is no possibility of their being said now. In the agony of his death, Jesus, too, will not be able to say, "In the very act of handing over my life to my Abba, with all the love of my heart I hand over my life to you and for you as well. I die not because my life is taken from me, wrenched from my hands. I freely and willingly break my own body for you; I myself pour out every drop of blood in my body for you." Instead of choosing to stay safely in his own land of Galilee, he makes the enormous decision to go to Jerusalem one last time. Here he will greet his death with love.

At the passover feast he joins the company of other Jews who will celebrate the feast in Jerusalem. Here Jesus gathers his loved ones around him to eat together the paschal meal celebrating the mercies of Yahweh given in the Hebrews' Exodus from Egypt. Jesus celebrates the ritual meal according to ancient traditions, but at the pivotal moment when the head of the family would pass around the bread and cup, Jesus makes a radical departure with the ritual. Instead of simply sharing the bread and wine in communion with the Jews freed by Yahweh's loving kindness from Egypt's slavery long ago, Jesus makes of this sharing a means of drawing together past, present, and future in a poignant gesture and gift of love. He makes of this last supper with his loved ones before his death a true eucharist, a living act of thanksgiving to his Abba which sums up and makes present the entire meaning of his life as it culminates in the self-giving of his death.

He takes the bread into his hands, and before passing it to his friends, he blesses it, breaks it, and in the very act of breaking the bread speaks the meaning of this gesture: "This is my body broken for you." He takes the cup of wine and, as it is shared among the apostles, again speaks the profound new meaning of this gesture: "This is my blood which will be poured out for you."

In this last supper, Jesus anticipates in a poignant act of love his death on the cross before it happens; he makes his own death present in a symbolic way that actually effects what it symbolizes. As Jacques Guillet has emphasized, Jesus does not simply take the bread and *point* to it while saying the words, "This is my body." No, he takes the bread and *breaks* it, and in the very act of breaking the bread says, "This is my body broken for you."[2] At the moment of his excruciating death on the cross, Jesus will not be able to say the meaning of his tortured death. He will not be able to cry out, "No one takes my life from me. I freely *give* it; I myself break my body for you; I myself pour out my blood for you."

On the cross he will be unable to do anything except to strain for the next gasp of air. But his loved ones will know because of this very meal that no one has wrested his life from him; he himself freely gives himself in an act of unconditional love that sums up the entire meaning of his life.

In breaking the bread, Jesus breaks his own body, and in pouring out the wine, pours out his own blood for the sin of the world.

2. The Crucifixion

We derive the word "excruciating" from "crucifixion," the hideously tortured death the Romans had used for hardened criminals and enemies of the state. Jewish zealots, rebels who incited riots against foreign rule, were crucified as an effective way to discourage others with similar intentions. The Romans would hardly have been interested in Jesus as the center of what they considered to be religious squabbles among the Jews. And so the Jewish leaders—who were not permitted to put anyone to death themselves—succeeded in convincing the Romans that Jesus was such a zealot. This is the point of the sarcastic inscription above the cross of Jesus: "Jesus of Nazareth, King of the Jews." Crucifixion was death by asphyxiation. Jesus was beaten and spikes were driven into his wrists and ankles so that his torn arms and legs had to support the entire weight of his body. Every gasp for air caused extreme agony, for it demanded that Jesus pull his entire weight upwards simply to take the next tortured breath. This would continue for hours until his arms and legs could not support the weight of his body, and, no longer able to breathe, he would die of strangulation.

But it was not finally asphyxiation that killed Jesus. More than physical pain the sense of being alone and abandoned is the ultimate torture in any of our sufferings. At times like this, when we feel as if we are hanging from a fraying rope over a chasm ready to swallow us up, we have an intimation that the essence of hell is isolation. In his own death Jesus enters into these depths of our human experience, into abandonment and betrayal: "My God, my God, why have you forsaken me?" And yet, in doing so, he cries out with a last action which gathers together the entire meaning of his life. He submits himself not only to the mystery of his Abba's will but also to the mystery of our human existence, to its tortured doubts and anxiety and isolation. In spite of his own terror, his own uncertainty, Jesus surrenders himself in an infinite act of trust into the chasm that looms out to devour his life. To the pit over which he hangs Jesus cries out, "Abba." "My Father, I surrender myself to you. I abandon myself to the chasm of death; in its depths I trust that I will find you yourself, and that the unbreakable force of your love will make me live again."

Jesus therefore faces the hatred hurled against him not only with unconditional trust but also with unconditional love. His hands are held fast, his feet pinned to the cross; his very posture speaks a love that will reject no one, a love that will not walk away. His figure is a silent, poignant contrast to our own reactions. We know what it is to be like boxers, using our hands to strike back emotionally and physically, accusing and blaming others, fighting hurt with hurt. We know, too, what it is figuratively to use our feet to retaliate, to treat others as if they did not exist, to take revenge by withdrawing.

Yet this is not the posture of Jesus. The people taunt him: "If this is God's Son, let him show it and come down from the cross" (Mt 27:40). But Jesus stretches his arms on the cross in an embrace rather than in retaliation, letting his body speak what his words now could not: "I will not strike out against you, even if you should kill me." His feet nailed to the wood say what his mouth no longer has the strength to say: "I will not go away from you; I will not withdraw my love from you. Your sin and death itself will not make me leave you." Jesus is not bound to the wood by the force of the spikes which rip open his wrists and ankles. As Catherine of Siena knew, love alone held Jesus fastened to the instrument of his death. No nail could be made strong enough to hold the Son of God on the cross had his own love not held him there.[3]

E. HOW THE DEATH OF JESUS HAS SAVED US

Jesus' death culminates the meaning of his life in one final act of lavish, unconditional love. But how and why is it precisely this death of Jesus that, according to our basic Christian confession, "saves us"? And what does such a death have to do with our confession of faith in a triune God?

We must first ask what it means to be saved. "Original sin" is our experience of living with minds and hearts and bodies that are in varied ways wounded by a propensity to act from selfishness rather than from self-giving love. Original sin is our experience of living in a world where it is unquestionably easier for us to hurt and strike out than it is for us to love and forgive one another. We know what it is to see one person's hurt and anger start a chain reaction volatile enough to provoke an entire household into lashing out against one another. The words "original sin" refer to this kind of experience of alienation and inner division so much a part of human life itself.

Caught up in a chain reaction of selfishness, we pass our own inner wounds on to others. This is the "sin of the world," the web of hurt and bitterness, of pride and domination which, in spite of all of the love and good in the world, keeps on incarnating itself in our midst from the dawn of human history until now. We derive the word "salvation" from the Latin word *salvus,* connoting healing and wholeness. "Salvation" would mean the gracious experience of having this chain reaction broken. It would mean experiencing life within us not as destructive drives of hatred and bitterness, not as the forces of anger and selfishness destroying us and those around us, but as the inner wellness and wholeness that come from love and peace.

And if there were someone who would let all of the hatred and bitterness of the world be hurled against him or her, absorb it into his or her own person, and instead of striking out again would return only unconditional love, the web of the world's hurt and hate would be broken in this one person alone. But is there any one of us capable of this kind of response to the "sin of the world?" Our own experience teaches us that we may be kind and generous and forgiving under many and even most circumstances, but there are limits to our capacity to love. Pushed far enough we will retaliate, or withdraw.

It is not we who are capable of absorbing the world's bitterness and responding with love. Only God can love with this kind of love. And this is precisely what happens in the death of Jesus. All of the forces of evil throughout history gather together at this moment to crush under their weight one who is love itself in human flesh. Yet Jesus will not go away, and he will not strike back.

He stretches his torn body upon the wood of the cross and surrenders himself to those who hate him. On this cross love itself absorbs the world's hatred and evil into its vast embrace, and here in this embrace, the chain of hurting passed on throughout all of history is broken. This is the meaning of the poignant words of John 13:1, as the author begins the account of the Last Supper. On the night he was betrayed, "having loved his own . . . he loved them to the end." "To the end. . .," that is, not only to the very end of his life, but to the very end of the limits that love can go.

We know what it is to experience betrayal, perhaps a betrayal so treacherous that years later we still feel the force of its bitterness. The gift we once made of ourselves in love and trust has been thrown back in our face. If we could, we would take back what we had so trustingly given, for only a fool would willingly bestow the treasure of herself or himself in the full knowledge that this self-giving would have no outcome except ridicule and rejection. We find ourselves betrayed precisely because we never thought we would be.

"On the night he was betrayed, . . . having loved his own, Jesus loved them to the end," to the very limits that love can go. Jesus needs no divine omniscience to read the hearts of his friends and to see that he will be betrayed not by strangers or acquaintances but by the ones closest and dearest to him. He knows ahead of time that his unreserved self-giving will be thrown back in his face, and by the very ones he has trusted with his life. And yet Jesus still gives himself without reserve, without holding anything back, and to the very ones he knows will desert him. His every action as he approaches death says to them: "I give myself to you ahead of time, even as I know you will prove faithless. I give myself to you more fully and freely than if you were never going to betray me. Not even your treachery will make me take my love from you or lessen the force of its gift and extent." "Having loved his own, he loved them to the end." Here, finally, in Jesus' unconditional love we have a power for our own human wholeness.

Yet we must ask whether Jesus could have broken the chain of hurting inextricable from our history by just one human breath filled with love. Why and how is it that we are saved precisely by his death? We know that no mere example of love given in return for hatred can save us, that no example can be a power for wholeness within us; it can be only a model outside of us, pointing to how we *should* live, but powerless to effect that kind of life within us. Truly human salvation would mean a power for love that is truly ours, truly human, a power not simply outside us but within us. And it would also mean a power for love which would invade and permeate every part of our being and every experience of our life.

Jesus does not simply enter into one isolated human experience and in this one experience return only love. In the death which sums up his entire life, Jesus freely plunges himself also and finally into the one experience no human person can escape, into the forces that will attack and devour, and at the end destroy every one of us. And precisly in this way he enters into the depths of *every* possible human experience. For in the death of Jesus, it is not simply an innocent person but infinite love itself who dies a violent death at the hands of human hatred. Jesus freely gives himself not simply to the hands of death, but to a death so monstrous that it will take into its grasp every cruel torment, every unjust and violent death that has ever happened in human history or ever will.

From within these depths filled with heinous atrocities, a death which has the power to evoke from us only bitterness and rage, Jesus responds with a *yes* of infinite self-giving. In an unspeakable act of trust which sums up his entire life, he calls this pit, "Abba," and surrenders himself with all of the love of his heart into its darkness. In the very act of doing so, he pours out upon the face of the universe in response to our human hatred a power of love unheard of in human history.

Now there is real power for *us*. Our salvation, our human wholeness, requires a truly *human yes* to God's unreserved self-giving. But our own experience teaches us that no one of us is capable by ourselves of this kind of absolute self-giving. The whole meaning of the inherent human weakness which we call original sin is that we resist and reject love, that we are so many times a human *no* to God and one another rather than an unreserved *yes*. The paradox is that it takes more than one who is human to respond without reserve in a fully human way; it takes God to be fully human, to give a fully human *yes*. In an inconceivable gift of love to us, the triune God makes present in our human history the very reality at the heart of the divine life. Jesus gives his entire person to the Father in a fully human *yes;* the human flesh which in us has throughout our history so often met hatred with hatred now in him pours itself out in a love without reserve.

F. THE PASCHAL MYSTERY: RESURRECTION, ASCENSION, PENTECOST

1. Resurrection and Ascension

"After this, Jesus knowing that all was now finished … bowed his head and gave up his spirit" (Jn 19:28, 30). For the author of John, the crucifixion is the event of Jesus' supreme self-giving. In this moment lies the heart of Jesus' passage to unending risen life, life which will break forth from his torn human flesh in the lavish outpouring of the Holy Spirit, the very person of love. The crucifixion is thus one facet of Jesus' total paschal mystery, his passover to infinite life through his death, resurrection, ascension, and pentecost. The author of John thus sees this moment of the crucifixion as simultaneously the outpouring of the Holy Spirit and therefore also of the radical transformation that is his resurrection. Before his resurrection, the pre-risen human flesh of Jesus could only "contain" the Holy Spirit. But in the act of self-giving that is his death, this same Spirit of unreserved love breaks forth into the very flesh of Jesus, so permeating him that in his still human but now transformed, risen flesh, Jesus becomes *Lord, giver* of the Spirit.

The resurrection of Jesus, therefore, is not a mere resuscitation, restoring to Jesus simply the same kind of limited existence he had before his death. Rather, the mystery of his resurrection means that in his very flesh the Holy Spirit's power and brilliance break forth, effecting a human transformation in him so all-encompassing that the Spirit who filled Jesus now breaks forth even into his body. In his risen human flesh Jesus becomes *giver* of the Spirit. This is why the resurrection of Jesus is finally pentecost; to encounter the risen Lord *is* to receive the Holy Spirit.

What, then, is the meaning of the ascension? In his Acts of the Apostles, Luke portrays the deepest theological meaning of the ascension as the exaltation of Jesus in his risen humanity. Luke pictures Peter preaching to the crowds on pentecost, the day on which the apostles' first public proclamation of Jesus as risen Lord results in a lavish bestowal of the Spirit. "This Jesus God raised up, and of that we all are witnesses. Being therefore exalted at the right hand of God, and having received from the Father the promise of the Holy Spirit, he has poured out that which you see and hear" (Acts 2:32-33).

The feast of the ascension is thus the feast of the exaltation of our human flesh in Jesus. In him we will forever adore God made flesh; through him we will gain the fulfillment of our own destiny, the radiant transformation of our own human bodies. The ascension celebrates the risen human Jesus adored as God at the right hand of the Father and because of this all the more intimately present within and among us. The resurrection and ascension, therefore, do not mean that Jesus floats up to heaven and now lives there, waiting for us to come home. On the contrary, the resurrection and ascension mean that, *because* of his risen flesh, Jesus is present to us even more intimately than ever before. In his pre-risen body, limited by time and space, only a few people could be near Jesus at any one time. But at the resurrection of Jesus, his utterly transformed, risen body is permeated with the glory and beauty of the Holy Spirit, transcending the limitations of time and space, filling the universe, and enabling Jesus as risen Lord to live within us.

Because of Jesus, we, too, will know a resurrection which completely transforms our human existence; like that of Jesus, our risen bodies also will not know the limitations of time and space. Now we often experience the pain of not being truly present to one another; our bodies are in one place, while our minds are far away. In our risen existence, however, our task will not be as it is now, to put our minds where our bodies are. It will be, rather, to put our bodies where our minds are; because of our transformed existence, we will be where our minds take us.

In the resurrection we have a power for human transformation even now and can see the signs of this power at work not only in others' lives but also on their faces. We may know people whose faces radiate a peace and joy that make their skin seem almost transparent with a light that breaks through from within their whole being onto their faces. The eastern churches, in particular, have a profound intuition of the risen Lord's glory already transfiguring the bodies of those who love him.

Through his resurrection made present in faith to us, a resurrection which is not only the exemplar but also the very source and cause of our own, Jesus thus gives us even now a transformed existence free from limitations in the deepest sense, an existence lived in the power of unlimited love. Jesus merges his risen humanity with our own, becoming the human power within us for our own *yes* to God even now: "I have been crucified with Christ; it is no longer I who live, but Christ who lives in me; and the life I now live in the flesh I live by faith in the Son of God who loved me and gave himself for me" (Gal 2:20). Now there is truly a *human* power that is also God's power in us.

We need to ask, however, why it is so crucial that the source of our salvation be truly human. We know that salvation requires our human wholeness, a truly human *yes* within us. As one of my own students commented, human salvation is not simply God within us saying *yes* to God, but we ourselves saying *yes* to God. Because Jesus' risen humanity is now merged with ours—and this is the whole meaning of his resurrection—we do have within us human power for our wholeness, but fully human power precisely because it is the humanness of one who is divine.

2. Pentecost

What happened to the apostles themselves in their own experience of the resurrection? With Raymond Brown we can conjecture that after the crucifixion the apostles, frightened and confused, fled Jerusalem. They are from Galilee, and they have no desire to stay in the large city of Jerusalem to find out whether they will suffer the same fate as their master. But on their way home to Galilee, Jesus, risen and glorious, encounters them. What was this encounter like? It is not that the apostles could see the human risen body of the Lord, for his transformed existence transcends the limitations of time and space and exceeds all that our meager sight can contain or perceive. We can surmise, however, that Jesus made himself known by some visible manifestation so that the apostles could recognize his new presence with them. Thus the interim resurrection "appearances" recounted by the Gospels were some form of external manifestation coupled with the central dimension of an interior, life-changing encounter with Jesus, risen Lord of the universe.[4]

In these encounters, which could have lasted one day as well as the symbolic forty days spoken of by Luke in Acts, the apostles' fear and shame at their cowardice and betrayal come face to face with Jesus' forgiving love. Downcast and remorseful, they are suddenly flooded with healing forgiveness by their Lord who now lives! In the power of this encounter, they continue to Galilee and remain there for a while, their courage growing to make the journey back to Jerusalem where their Lord had met his death. They decide to return for the next Jewish feast, pentecost, a harvest festival lasting seven weeks and celebrating the Sinai covenant.

In contrast to Luke, the author of John sees the paschal mystery as one event with multiple phases: Jesus' death, resurrection, ascension, pentecost. He tells of the apostles' pentecost as happening on the same day as the resurrection, the first day of the week. "On the evening of that day, the first day of the week . . . Jesus came and . . . breathed on them, and said to them, 'Receive the Holy Spirit'" (Jn 20:19, 22). Thus the apostles' own pentecost is this moment when they first encounter their risen Lord.

But the Acts of the Apostles tells of another pentecost, the outpouring of the Spirit at the apostles' preaching of the risen Lord in Jerusalem, as they celebrate the Jewish harvest festival of pentecost. During the Jewish feast itself, the first-fruits of the crops were offered to God on the first day of the festival, and the rest of the crop on the last day. Luke sees in this Hebrew feast a symbol of the early Christian experience of the Spirit: on the "first" day of the new pentecost (the day of the resurrection), Jesus, first-fruits of the resurrection, is offered to the Father; on the last, the "fiftieth" day (Luke's pentecost), all of the rest of the "crop," the entire people of God, receive the outpouring of the Spirit from their risen Lord.

Because the glorious risen body of the Lord fills the universe with the Spirit "not by measure" (Jn 3:43) but lavishly, Luke portrays in nearly every succeeding chapter of Acts the sense of the excitement and new life which the continued outpouring of the Spirit effects among the early communities. "When they had prayed, the place where they had gathered together was shaken and they were all filled with the Holy Spirit and spoke the word of God with boldness" (Acts 4:31). Their own experience of the transforming power of Jesus' resurrection, of having their own lives utterly changed and turned upside down, is thus absolutely central in the early Christians' proclamation of the Gospel.

With the Holy Spirit poured out upon them, they begin to experience the power of Jesus' resurrection in their lives. The more they ask for the Spirit of Jesus, the more this Spirit is lavished upon them (Lk 11:13), filling the preachers and those who hear them with forgiveness and confidence, with reconciliation and peace. In turn, still others are drawn by the same power of the Gospel as they see in their midst people's lives being radically changed. As they try to articulate the source of the transformation they are undergoing, they cannot separate their experience of the risen Lord and his Spirit's outpouring of new life and love among then, drawing them together into a true community of brothers and sisters.

The Acts of the Apostles and epistles make clear that in their proclamation and hearing of the Gospel, in their initiation of new members into the community, in their celebration of the eucharist, something really *happened* for the early Christians. An overwhelming sense of the *power* of the risen Lord in his Holy Spirit filled them; they *experienced* the force of a divine love that is triune, the strength of the Spirit whom their Father continued to pour out upon them from the risen flesh of their Lord, making new their own lives and that of their families.

The early Christians in this way experienced the mysteries of the crucifixion, resurrection, ascension, and pentecost as no mere doctrines but the very transforming energy of a gratuitous divine love within them, giving them a whole new way to exist in communion with God and one another. Jesus' unreserved self-giving on the cross to his Abba and to us in this way has made intimately and irrevocably present in our human history the very reality at the heart of the triune God, and has unleashed upon the entire created cosmos the power of its radiance.

3

Speaking the Experience: Attempts at Articulation

We have reflected on the meaning of Jesus' paschal mystery as the source of our faith in the triune God. We turn now to consider the most significant of the Christian community's past and present efforts to articulate more deeply the identity of the Trinity. In this chapter, therefore, after reflecting on both the limitations and yet necessity of our speaking about the tri-personal God, we present an overview of trinitarian thought through the ages. Our reflections center on the contributions of early councils, key patristic writers, medieval thinkers such as Aquinas, and representative contemporary Christian theologians.

A. THE DIGNITY AND INADEQUACY OF SPEAKING ABOUT GOD

1. Our Human Need to Speak of God

Our reflections on the importance of the community's faith articulations lead us first to consider both the inadequacy and value of our attempts to express the identity of the triune God. Whenever we have had a deep experience that awakens and radically changes us, we feel urged to speak about it in some way, to say it and share it with another. Yet in our attempts to express what we have experienced, we frequently end by saying

"I cannot put this into words." In the presence of mysteries like birth and love and death, words fail us and often bring us instead to a silent communion with one another before the very mystery we have tried to articulate.

We experience this radical inadequacy of human words even more when we try to speak of the triune God who infinitely exceeds all that we could think or imagine, and with whom we enter into communion through love rather than through language. Yet, as the early Christians knew, we are human persons created not only with hearts that thirst for the infinitely lovable but also with minds that hunger for the infinitely knowable. Nothing less than the triune God is the inexhaustible banquet on which both our hearts and our minds have been made to feast. Faith thus inescapably pushes us to theology, to seeking a deeper understanding and articulation of our belief in the triune God who is our source and goal.

It is one thing to experience a profound reality, however, and quite another to articulate it. We must use language to speak to and about God, but because the triune God infinitely exceeds everything which even the most brilliant created mind could grasp or express, every word we speak about God is immeasurably more unlike than like God. Finally, all of our ideas and words, no matter how exalted, stand dumb before the absolute mystery of God.

But even though we can only stammer about God with our words, our very nature and dignity as human beings nevertheless demand that we at least try. We *must* speak of the mystery which bathes our universe in love, in warmth and joy, in peace and light. The more we give the triune God the worship not only of our hearts, but also of our minds as well, the more God is glorified with a glory that is not God's need but rather ours. We achieve our highest self-actualization by freely entrusting ourselves in an unreserved worship of both our hearts and minds to the God who has been so unconditionally surrendered to us. To speak about the mystery of God transforming our lives is in this way not a peripheral exercise in semantics, but an expression of our deepest human fulfillment.

Paradoxically, when we ponder and speak of God's mystery, we come to gain more deeply who we ourselves are. For we speak not of a mystery unrelated to us, existing in the far-off heavens, but rather of the very ground and goal of our own identities. On the one hand, because our words are more untrue than true of God we have to deny all that we have taken such painful care to affirm. But it is also true that in our human stammering we express our highest dignity as human persons, and in this way give glory to the triune God.

2. *Ways of Speaking about God*

Although our ideas and words can never contain the infinite identity of God, in our various ways of speaking about God we do employ images, symbols and ideas drawn from our own human experience. We use symbol when we speak of God with words and images that touch us at a profound level of our human experience and in a way that evokes a depth response that cannot be easily articulated, for example, "God is Abba." We use theological metaphor when we bring together two meanings not usually associated with one another and in a way that creates a third, new meaning with the power to shock and awaken us in some way, for example, "Jesus is the light of the world."

Symbol and metaphor are valuable because of their poetic and evocative nature; however, like all human ways of speaking, they say more what God is *not,* rather than what God is. The first divine person, for example, is not a male nor light, nor any created thing. God is thus unspeakably more *unlike* a human father and even more *unlike* light than like either of these two created realities.

A third way we can speak about God is through analogy, language that uses concepts not tied to only one limited way of existing. In metaphor, the created limitation is built into the word itself; light, for example, has existence only as created reality. Analogy, in contrast, employs transcendental concepts like goodness, love, truth, and being. While unable to contain or grasp the inexhaustible treasure of God, these concepts are nevertheless open to a boundless way of existing. Since we know truth and goodness only through created beings that are true and good, we have no idea what uncreated goodness or truth might be. But the very openness of the concepts themselves to an unlimited way of existing at least points us in the true direction in which God's own infinite reality lies and so gives us a miniscule *intimation* of what God is like.[1]

A legend told of Augustine illustrates the inadequacy of our words before the triune God's inexhaustible depths. As Augustine walked along a beach contemplating what he would write about the Trinity, he encountered an angel in the guise of a small child. The child was trying to scoop the ocean into a small hole in the sand. When Augustine expressed incredulity at this futile task, the child responded that containing the entire ocean in a tiny hole in the sand was more possible than what Augustine himself was trying to do—capture the infinite treasures of the triune God in the tiny recesses of his own mind.

Speaking of God's mystery thus leads us ultimately to our knees, to silent adoration and communion with the very God of whom we speak. And when we do speak, we realize further our need to complement a "kataphatic" approach, making positive statements about God—for example, the triune God is beauty, truth, goodness itself—with an "apophatic" approach, denying at the same time that the triune God is beauty or truth or goodness in any of the created ways that we could experience of even imagine.

B. EARLY CHRISTIAN ARTICULATION OF THE TRIUNE GOD

We have reflected on both the dignity and radical inadequacy of our human language before the absolute mystery of God. We turn now to ask how we as a Christian community have developed a common heritage of articulations about the triune God. For though our proclamations and statements about God can be only meager and always deficient attempts to speak the unspeakable, nevertheless, they can open us to a deepening participation in the mystery of unconditional gift-love at the heart of the triune God.

1. The Christian Experience

The first Christians were Jews; in the midst of the polytheism around them, everything in them guarded the proclamation

that God is one alone. But like us, even as they entered wordlessly into communion with the God who had transformed
their lives, they had to speak in prayer to God and in communication with others of what they experienced. And as they
found their entire lives being transformed by the power of
Jesus' resurrection, they spontaneously began to call out in
praise and thanksgiving to the one they now experienced as
risen Lord in their midst.

In fidelity to their experience of Jesus' resurrection they *had*
to look for a radically new way to speak about and to God. In
their liturgy they spontaneously began to pray, as an "im-
mediate reflex" of their experiences, and "before all analysis of
its suitability," in a way that distinguished Jesus, his Abba,
and their Spirit.[2] The triune name thus capsulized the source
of their own experience of God as Christians, a God who did
wonders among them in a distinct, threefold way: "The Spirit
of him who raised Jesus will give life to your mortal bodies
also through his Spirit which dwells in you" (Rom 8:11);
"through Christ we have access in one Spirit to the Father"
(Eph 2:18).

They had known Jesus in the flesh; he had brought them
into the very presence of the transcendent God. The God
whose name, "Yahweh," they had not dared to pronounce,
Jesus had taught them to call by the intimate name of "Abba."
In his own tender love for them he had shown them what they
could never have dared even to imagine about the unspeakable
God of the universe: that their Abba loved them with the
gentleness of a mother nursing her child, with the strength and
tenderness of a father cradling his child in his arms. In Jesus
they had encountered the very presence of God. Yet they
realized that Jesus was not simply another name for "Abba,"
since it was to his Abba that Jesus always prayed. In this way
they began to know Jesus, their risen Lord, as the Father's
own gift to them, bringing the infinitely transcendent one
utterly close to them.

We know, however, that it takes more to make a gift than
simply the offer; even when it is held out to us, we can refuse
it. We can give our love to another and have it rejected; we can
close ourselves to the love which another lavishes upon us.
Perhaps one way the early Christians came to know the Holy

Spirit as distinct from both Jesus and their Abba was in this context, in their experience of a God who will not be refused. We ourselves cannot help wanting the reciprocality of a love freely offered and just as freely accepted and received. Yet even as we freely give, we cannot enter into the secret places of another's heart and forcefully wrest from it a *yes* to our self-giving. Nothing is as impossible as making someone love us; we are powerless to force open another's heart.

But when God gives a gift—especially the gift which is nothing less than *God*—the attraction and power freely to receive and accept it is built into this inestimable self-offer. With the gift, God also gives the inner, free *yes* to that gift, a *yes* which wells up spontaneously from the deepest recesses of our own being. Only God can effect in us the loving response which is truly our own because it comes from a source within us deeper even than our own power to say *no*. Their absolutely new life in Jesus taught the early Christians to know his Abba as their own. But they experienced the Father of Jesus as effective in the gift he bestows. This Abba gives not only the gift, his Son, but also the very power, joy, and delight to accept this gift, namely, the Holy Spirit binding them together in the bonds of *agape,* gift-love.

Our own experience of becoming vulnerable and then changed by love gives us an intimation of what these early Christians experienced. The gift bestowed from their Father through Jesus their risen Lord in the power of the Holy Spirit turned their lives upside down. In place of bitterness and resentment, the joy of forgiveness welled up in them, drawing them into a family where they finally belonged. Once isolated and alone, they had a whole new power to reach out in love. Anxiety and fear gave way to confidence and security in their own identity as God's sons and daughters.

In this way they surely began to experience Jesus as the gift, their Abba as the giver of the gift, and the Holy Spirit as the free and spontaneous *yes* within them to this gift. They experienced this living *yes,* this bond of love and communion among them, not simply as an impersonal force but truly as *someone,* the Spirit poured out among them through Jesus' resurrection.

They developed at this stage, very likely in an unreflexive

way, a baptismal liturgy which spontaneously expressed their experience of God and gave new members conscious access to this same God, "Father, Son, and Holy Spirit."[3] Their baptismal formula thus became the primal context for the community's explicit confession of faith in the triune God whose wonders they witnessed among them.

2. Jewish-Christian Thought Categories

As Jews still very much consecrated to the truth of their faith, the earliest Christians daily recited the *Shema,* "Hear O Israel, the Lord your God is one alone"(Deut 4:6). Paradoxically, however, their own Hebrew scriptures which so insist upon the oneness of God prepared them to find words which would articulate their experience of the identity of Jesus, his Abba, and their Holy Spirit poured out among them. According to these scriptures, God's word and wisdom permeate the earth with loving providence and care (Gen 1; Ps 33:6; Is 31:3; Wis 1:7; Ps 104:29); God's Spirit fills the universe with life, raises the dead and brings into being what is not (Ez 37). The early Christians spontaneously began to see Jesus as God's own wisdom and word in person, and the Spirit of Jesus as God's own Spirit in person, bathing the world in the healing power of the resurrection.

Two early developments among others helped to pave the way toward this new way of thinking about and expressing the source and content of their Christian experience. At this early stage, to call Jesus explicitly "God," *theos,* was unthinkable since the early community strongly adhered to their Jewish monotheism. *Theos* was for them Jesus' Abba. Yet in the translation of the Hebrew Scriptures used by the Greek-speaking Jewish Christians, the word *Kyrios,* "Lord" was used for the unpronounceable sacred Hebrew name, "Yahweh." As these early Jewish Christians were increasingly expelled from worship in the synagogue, they developed their own liturgies in which they spontaneously began to address Jesus, their risen Lord, as *Kyrios.*

In addition, Greek-speaking Jews found a meeting point with pagan Greeks in the term *logos,* denoting the principle of order and rationality in the universe. Hellenistic Jews, on the other hand, used *logos* to translate the Hebrew *dabar,* denoting God's creative "word" in history. Hellenistic Jewish Christians then began to use the word *logos* of Jesus. He is in person the living principle making sense of all creation as well as the living Word active in history and creating all things new through his resurrection.

"In the beginning was the Word, and the Word was with God, and the Word was God (*theos*)" (Jn 1:1). With time, the early Christians used the word *logos* to articulate their growing understanding of Jesus' identity not only as the Lord who will come at the end-time, at the parousia, not only as the present risen Lord in our midst, but also as the one who always has been the pre-existent, personal Word of God. This and other New Testament texts about the pre-existent Word are meant to convey not a sense of *time* before creation, but rather a sense of the "depth dimension" in Jesus, an "existence mysteriously transcending the limits of time and space": in him and in the events of his life, no one less than God acts.[4]

3. A Turning Point: Christian Faith in Greek Categories

Jerusalem did not long remain the womb of the Christian community. The destruction of this city in 70 A.D. by Romans quelling a Jewish insurrection resulted in a widespread diaspora of both Jews and Christian Jews to Greek-speaking cities of the Roman empire. Since Greek culture dominated the empire, this emigration from its Jewish matrix marked a radical turning point for Christianity.

As non-Jews became interested in the Christian faith, communities were pushed to find new ways to think and speak meaningfully to their pagan contemporaries about their Christian experience. Their own Hebrew heritage had given them a concrete, existential, experiential way of thinking. Now their mission to the whole world put them in dialogue with pagans and with the abstract, theoretical way of thinking characteristic of the Greeks.

The struggle of the community to find words to speak the mystery they had experienced in a way meaningful to their Greek contemporaries and without distorting it into falsehood lasted at least four hundred years. The Greek memory of their own historical origins stood in sharp contrast to the Hebrew and Jewish Christian experience. Only after the Jews had escaped from a slavery that allowed them to invade and conquer lands not theirs, did they themselves become a nation. They could attribute the miracle of this feat accomplished by nomad tribes only to a God actively involved in their affairs. Following upon their Hebrew heritage, Jewish Christians experienced the triune God intimately active in and involved with their history through the resurrection of Jesus.

Greece, on the other hand, became a nation as a result of invasion by Dorian tribes which devastated Mycenaean land and culture. In such a "national experience of sheer irrational contingency," the Greeks developed a theology of God in negative terms, a God who is the radical opposite of human contingency, one who is the immovable ground of all that is; the timeless, impassible, invisible, indescribable, intangible, imparticipable God absolutely removed from all human vicissitudes. This way of thinking about God made a third category of reality essential, mediators half way between the human and divine who could "bridge the gap" between a changeless God and continually changing human beings.[5]

Converted Greek Christians always faced the temptation of seeing Jesus as this kind of half-divine, half human mediator, either not fully God or not fully human. Influenced by a dualism that viewed spirit alone as good and matter as evil, docetists on the one hand taught that Jesus only appeared to be human and to die on the cross. On the other hand, subordinationists like Arius, a fourth-century priest of Alexandria, found it impossible to confess Jesus as truly God.

Arius could think of God only as the self-enclosed, imparticipable one whose nature by definition cannot be shared. If Jesus is truly God, either the Father's nature is shared and the Father is not God, or there are two gods. Arius drew the only logical conclusion he could within his Platonic framework: Jesus is the highest of a subordinate hierarchy of beings descending from the unoriginate Father, the only God. Jesus is not *homoousios,* of the same nature as the Father, but is rather God's highest creature.

Arius thus taught that Jesus is not of the "same substance" as the Father, that he is of an entirely different, created order.

Yet if our words are in the end inadequate, why did it matter what Arius said? As early Christians knew, if Jesus is not God, we are not saved; there is no power of transformation for our humanity. And if we cannot say in words the whole truth of God, at least we can say, "God is *not* this." At least we can say what deforms the content of our Christian experience. God's triuneness does *not* mean simply three different names for the exact same reality, the Father putting on three different hats or names (modalism), nor does it mean three separate gods (tritheism). Nor does it mean Arius' subordinationism.

4. The Councils of Nicaea and Constantinople

Gathered at Nicaea in 325 A.D. at Constantine's invitation and expense, Church leaders had to respond to Arius' teaching using his own terminology. Thus the creed formulated at Nicaea and which we profess each Sunday proclaims the Christian faith not only in scriptural categories but also in Greek ones. Into a baptismal confession of faith in the "Father, Son, and Holy Spirit" are inserted these proclamations about Jesus in response to Arius: Jesus is "God from God, light from light, true God from true God, begotten, not made, of the same substance (*homoousios*) with the Father."

While we must acknowledge the difficulty, if not impossibility, of uncovering the exact meaning of the word *homoousios* after so many centuries and in such a differing historical context as our own, nevertheless, we can say that the council does give new meaning to a Greek term, *ousia,* denoting the concrete substance or nature that something is. The council members use it to convey the truth that Jesus is divine, not a creature. Yet neither is Jesus the Father. He is God *from* God the Father. He is the divine Word, now become also fully human, who eternally comes from the Father in a non-material manner, the way light comes from light. Jesus is distinct from the Father since as Word he comes eternally from the Father, but he is not a creature; he is begotten, not made. The council members do not define what the word "begotten" *does* mean, for, as Gregory Nazianzen will later stress, we cannot know or say its meaning. But they do make clear what the word does *not* mean: origin in time or subordination to the origin. Finally, the council proclaims that Jesus is not another, second God, but the very same God as the Father: of the same substance—*homoousios*—as the Father.

Since so many eastern Christians had been influenced by Arius' subordinationism, the Church struggled to clarify the meaning and to gain acceptance of its faith confession for at least the next five decades. Part of the continuing struggle involved recognizing also the divinity and unique personal identity of the Holy Spirit. Arian "pneumatomachians" or "Spirit-fighters" were teaching that the Spirit is an impersonal, created force. In an attempt to unite the church as Constantine had done, the emperor Theodosius I convoked the Council of Constantinople in 381.

Again, as the early community realized, if the Spirit is not God, there is no power for us flowing from Jesus' resurrection, no way to participate in the very life of God. Under the theological leadership of Gregory Nazianzen, church leaders proclaimed the Holy Spirit's identity as "Lord and Giver of Life" who "proceeds from the Father" (Jn 15:26), and added this confession to the creed of Nicaea. In this way they confessed the personal identity, distinction and divinity of the Holy Spirit but at the same time tried to escape the long-term theological entanglements which the use of philosophical words like *homoousios* had occasioned five decades earlier.

C. PATRISTIC REFLECTION

1. *The Cappadocians*

During the fourth century, the eastern "Cappadocians," Basil the Great, Gregory of Nyssa, and Gregory Nazianzus, were especially influential in reworking several Greek concepts for proclamation about the triune God's identity. They used the term *ousia* to denote the triune God's one same nature, *what* God is—the ocean of life and truth, being and goodness itself—and the term *hypostasis* to denote *who* the Father, Son and Spirit are as distinct.

Yet what does it mean to say that God is three "hypostases," since God is certainly not three "persons" in any way that we experience, namely, as separate bodily individuals with separate consciousness. Again, it is difficult if not impossible to get at the precise content of the word "hypostasis" for the Cappadocians, just as it is in the case of the Latin term used by Tertullian, *persona*. But we can try to approach as nearly as possible the context which prompted the use of these terms. Aristotle had distinguished between substance, what exists in itself and is denoted by a noun (candles, trees, persons) and accidents, described with an adjective (brown, pretty, tall) which exist not in themselves but only in a substance, and therefore, like the brownness of hair, can cease to be.

In the context of these categories, the Arians posed this question to the Christians: "The God you confess as three persons must be either three substances or three accidents. If they are three separate substances, you are tritheists; and if they are three accidents, three different modes of one person, then only the Father is *really* God, just as we have been saying all along."

Nazianzen responded by giving a new meaning to the term "relation," which Aristotle had defined as an accidental quality. For Nazianzen, the divine persons are distinguished by their mutual relations to one another (*Oratio* 29, 16). Aquinas later draws upon this insight to show that *what* the Father, Son and Spirit are *is* the one divine nature which is to *be* life and goodness itself. But *who* each person is, is sheer *relation* to each other, in a way absolutely unknown to our own experience. The divine persons thus are not separate substances; neither, however, are they simply "accidental" qualities of or names for the Father who alone is God. They are unique persons distinguished precisely by their unique relation to one another. The Father alone is the first person, God *unbegotten,* source without source. The Son alone is second person, God eternally *begotten* from the Father in perfect equality. And the Spirit alone is third person, God eternally *proceeding* from the Father (Jn 15:23) in perfect equality. Neither the eastern church nor the Nicene-Constantinople creed formulated in the east confess the Spirit's procession from *both* Father and Son (*filioque*) as Augustine and the western Church after him would. Eastern theologians distinguished the Spirit simply by calling the Spirit the one who *proceeds* from the Father, while the Son is *begotten* of the Father; they viewed these two scriptural words as indefinable.

The early Church's struggle to articulate its trinitarian faith was not finished with the Councils of Nicaea and Constantinople. The school of Antioch traditionally focused on the humanity of Jesus, while the School of Alexandria stressed his divinity. In an attempt to safeguard Jesus' humanity, Nestorius, bishop of Antioch, explained his identity as a human person who exists in the divine person of the Word. Mary is the mother of Jesus but not of the divine Word and therefore cannot be called *theotokos,* "God-bearer," "Mother of God." Cyril of Alexandria and others interpreted Nestorius as teaching that Jesus is two persons, and in 431 a council at Ephesus proclaimed Jesus' identity as one divine person, God the Son, who has saved us precisely in becoming human at the Incarnation.

2. The Council of Chalcedon

Twenty years later, a monk of the Alexandrian tradition named Eutyches took the confession of Ephesus to its extreme by his monophysite ("one nature") understanding of Jesus' identity. Eutyches reduced Jesus' humanity to an illusion: Jesus has only one nature, the divine nature of the Father. In response to Eutyches and after complications involving theological correspondence between prominent bishops and Pope Leo the Great himself, the Council of Chalcedon in 451 articulated a confessional statement affirming that Jesus is one divine person with two natures, human and divine. He is *homoousios*—of the same nature—as the Father in his divinity, and *homoousios* with us in his humanity. This last great christological statement of the early church became authoritative, but also, as we shall see, for not a few contemporary theologians, problematic.[6]

3. Augustine

These developments occurred at the heart of eastern Christian reflection on the Trinity. In terms of western trinitarian insight, Augustine of Hippo (354-430) made his own lasting impact. Augustine himself was reluctant to use the term *per-*

sona of God. He writes that he does so not to affirm something but so that he will not say nothing in response to the question "Three what?" (*De Trinitate* 5, 9, 10). For insight into the Trinity, he reflects on our own individual consciousness and discovers there, as later psychologists like Freud and Jung also would, a three-fold structure. Augustine's analysis, however, functions to illumine his Christian faith. All of creation comes from the hands of the triune God, but our own beings especially are etched with the signs of our trinitarian origin. Our human psyche itself has an inherent threefold structure: memory, knowledge, and love. Because these powers to remember, to know, and to love not only ourselves but also God are truly distinct powers yet exist within the oneness of our own being, they give us an analogy for the unfathomable life of the triune God (*De Trinitate* 8, 10; 9, 2).

Again, our own experience of lover, beloved, and the very love uniting them gives us a small hint of the life of God: the Spirit is in person the bond of love uniting Father and Son as lover and beloved. As the very person of their love and communion, the Spirit necessarily proceeds eternally from *both* Father and Son—*filioque*—(*De Trinitate* 4, 20; 5, 11; 5, 14). By means of this last insight, Augustine hoped to articulate more clearly why the Spirit is truly distinct from the Son who also comes eternally from the Father. Eventually Augustine's *filioque* was inserted into the Nicene-Constantinople creed recited at Rome in the eleventh century and in this way became part of the doctrinal heritage of the western church—an action which provoked eastern denouncement and provided one reason for the schism between East and West in 1054.

D. MEDIEVAL SYNTHESIS: AQUINAS' CONTRIBUTION

The Dominican Thomas Aquinas (1224-1274) made a lasting impact on western trinitarian reflection by taking Augustine's psychological analogy to an even deeper philosophical level. His gifts as a creative thinker allowed him to use Aristotelian categories, give them an entirely new meaning when applied to God, and in this way provide a new depth of insight into the richness of the triune life. His focus on three key concepts—nature, processions, and the divine persons as relationships of love—continues to provide a rich source of reflection for contemporary trinitarian theology.

1. The Triune God's Nature as Sheer Existence

Aquinas viewed nature or essence as *what* we are, the source of our activity and consciousness; human nature is what delimits our person in the particularly human way of being in the world. As human persons with a human nature, we *have* life and existence. To be *God,* however, is not to *have* a nature as a source of activity; the triune God's very essence or nature is *to be* existence, to be the ocean of life itself. There is no hint or shadow of separateness and division in *what* each divine person is, for *what* one is, all are, namely, the one same infinite life and beauty and goodness itself.

This is why every love story in the universe draws its ground and meaning from the love story at the heart of God. Love means union with another, and there is no union in the cosmos as profound as the union of Father, Son, and Spirit. As created persons, we ourselves have separate minds and wills. No matter how much we love, the best we can do is to strive for communion with someone who remains always separate from us. Our own love for one another thus can only be an attempt to bridge the separateness that we can never completely overcome simply because our distinct personhood means for us also separate natures, wills, minds, hearts, and lives. There is always that place within us which no one else can enter, and where we are a stranger even to ourselves.

But the Father, Son, and Holy Spirit not only have but *are* the same will, mind, and consciousness, the one same life itself lived uniquely by three distinct subjects or persons. The utterly unique way that they *are* this one life constitutes them as absolutely distinct persons. The Father is life and goodness itself as Father; the Son is this same life itself as Son. And the Spirit, too, is this same life itself uniquely as the Spirit. The Son and Spirit are exactly *what* the Father is, without being *who* the Father is. Supreme mystery of personal distinctions in utter unity: each person is not a third of God, not a piece of life itself, but the *whole* of God, the *same* entirety of life and goodness itself, yet uniquely so.

Our own human nature gives us the capacity to do certain things: to know, to love, to laugh. As persons who exist, we give existence to our nature, to what we are. But we are not our own existence; there is no necessary reason for us to be. We only *have* existence, beauty, goodness, and love; we cannot say to one another, "You are love itself." And because we are beings who only have existence, we can lose it. There is, therefore, a true difference between *who* (person), *what* (nature), and *that* (existence) we are (*Summa Theologiae,* I, q. 54, a. 3).

The triune God, however, is not *a being* who *has* existence, a substance limited and circumscribed as we are, but the vast plentitude of *BE-ing,* of dynamic life and activity itself. To be God is to be existence itself, fullness of *be-ing.* For Thomas, God is *ipsum esse subsistens: to be* is the very nature of God. God does not *have* love or goodness or beauty or life; God *is* goodness and beauty, the infinite ocean of life itself, but not as an impersonal force. The triune God is what it means to be life itself as *someone,* as the infinite richness of person (*Summa Theologiae,* I, qq. 3-26).

All of creation exists only because it continually draws forth its life from the God who is the infinite sea of life itself. We drink the teaspoons of life that we *have* and that flow within us from the ocean of life that God *is.* We exist only because we draw all that we are and most deeply *that* we are at all from the vast ocean of *BE-ING* that God is. The triune God does not simply live within us; we live and move and literally *have our being* within the triune God.

But where does the triune God live? John tells us that the home of the Son is in the Father (Jn 1:18). Because they *are* the one same life, the Father, Son, and Spirit are inseparable; where one is, all three are. The divine persons live in one another; they are one another's home. To hint at this magnificent truth, Latin writers used the word *circumincession,* "walking around" in one another. But Greek theologians spoke instead of *perichoresis,* "dancing around," a word that suggests the dynamic activity and excitement it is to be *God* dwelling in God: the divine persons not only live in one another but also "dance" in one another.

2. Processions and Their Extension to Us in the Missions

The life of the triune God thus is not a static existence like that of a rock. We ourselves find it exhilarating to be alive, but the excitement it is to be God, to be *life itself,* transcends all that we could imagine. It is true that as created persons we do many activities, yet even our most precious and characteristically human activities, those of knowing and loving, and even breathing itself, are not identical with our life; they are only the effect of our life. But in God, knowing and loving are not simply occasional activities but essential actions identical with the very nature of God; it is not simply that God knows, but that the triune God *is* the divine knowing and loving.

Aquinas speaks of this dynamic life of God's Be-ing as flowing forth in processions—dynamic, interior activities of knowing and loving that stay within the very life of God and are one with that very life, and eternally so. When we ourselves know others, we have an idea or word of them within us, just as when we love them, we carry, as it were, an impression, a seal of them in our hearts. The fruit or term of our own knowing or loving is an idea or impression which, while existing within us, is distinct and separate from both who and what we are.

In God, however, the fruit or *term* of these two activities is nothing less than divine persons; as the known is in the knower and the beloved in the lover, the Son and Spirit are in the Father. Far from being external to God, the term of the Father's vibrant and ceaseless self-knowing, generation, *is* God the Son. This word is not *who* the Father is and yet completely expresses *what* the Father is. And the immanent term of the Father's eternally loving this Word is the living person of the Holy Spirit (*Summa Theologiae* I, qq. 27-38). Within God the dynamic activities of knowing and loving truly bear fruit not in something other than God but in two who are the very persons of God the Son and Holy Spirit (*Summa Theologiae* I, qq. 32-37).

This tremendous, ceaseless activity of knowing and loving within the very heart of God overflows in a created way to us in what Thomas and others have called the missions of the Son and Spirit (*Summa Theologiae* I, q. 43). We ourselves can give only what we have, for we possess even our life and very self only as a result of God's goodness to us. Yet the gifts of our creation, existence, and all that we are as human persons—what classical theology calls "nature"—as wonderful as these are, are infinitely surpassed by the far more gratuitous bestowal of grace, the created gift of sharing in the very life of God.

Through this absolutely undeserved gift, we human persons are no longer simply creatures but also *friends* and *intimates* of the triune God. In the life of grace, we receive finally nothing less than the very *self* of God in an intimate self-giving. The Son's eternal birth from the Father is extended outside of God to us in the incarnation, and the eternal breathing forth of the Spirit is extended to us in the experience of pentecost—missions which are the result only of God's grace to us. In the effusion of the triune God's love poured out on us through the missions, the very life of God is extended to us: the Son is given to us and the Spirit bestowed upon us.

Karl Rahner focuses on this insight, namely that the processions are continued in the missions, the sending of the Son and Spirit to us in our history, and develops as his basic axiom the insight that the economic Trinity *is* the immanent Trinity and vice versa.[7] Because the "economy" of salvation is the plan or history of our salvation centered in the missions of the Word and Spirit to us, the "economic" Trinity is the triune God acting among us to save and heal us. But the temporal sending of the Word and Spirit to us is an extension and prolongation into our history of the "immanent" Trinity, the triune God in the mystery of the inner divine life. There is, therefore, only one triune God; the "immanent" Trinity is the "economic" Trinity, that is, the Trinity who saves us, but this saving activity among us is a reflection of the triune God's own life.

Thus, the inner life of the Trinity is not a beautiful but esoteric mystery absolutely unrelated to how this same God is intimately present to us. What the triune God does for us, how God relates intimately with us, is also in some way who God truly is. Who God is always bears fruit in God's coming intimately to us, inviting us into the very love and communion of the inner divine life. Thus, Jesus is the infinitely beautiful

Word of the Father spoken into our midst, and the Spirit is the unspeakably joyful *yes* to this Word who is the Father's perfect self-expression from all eternity.

When we say that the processions are taking place eternally in God, we do not mean our present experience of time without end—little pieces of life measured out to us in teaspoonfuls of what has already happened, and what has not yet happened, each measure finished far too quickly in some cases, and far too slowly in others. The triune God, who is the ocean of inexhaustible life itself, does not live life in tiny teaspoons. Since God's life truly is *life*, eternity means the plentitude of triune life and love that is always now, that gives us nothing we will regret leaving, because there is nothing and no one we will ever have to leave.

The lavish activity at the heart of God transcends the limitations of all time and is "eternal," not accomplished once for all in some moment at the beginning of time but occurring always *now*. The Son is eternally being born from the heart of the Father, and the Father and Son are always breathing forth the Spirit of their love. In some mysterious way our own creation shares in the always *now* birth of the Word and breathing forth of the Spirit in God. And because this is so, we were not made once for all or just at our conception long ago; the triune God's love continually creates and sustains each of us at every moment.

3. The Divine Persons as Sheer Relationships

But what does it mean that *God* is three "persons"? In our own experience "person" means a separate individual capable of thinking and loving and entering into relationship. But to be person as God, radically transcends anything we know as person. Like Augustine, we apply the word "person" to the three who are God in order to hint at the unsurpassable truth that God is not *something,* to be used and manipulated, but *someone,* with whom we can be in relationship precisely because the divine persons *are* sheer subsistent relations to one another (*Summa Theologiae,* I, q. 29, a. 4).

Even as we say that the three who are God are subsistent relations, there is nothing in our own human experience which could capture what this might mean. It is true that each of us knows from experience what it means to thirst in some way for a person who would be totally *for us,* someone turned unreservedly toward us. We know, too, the pain of wounded or broken relationships and shattered hopes that a human person would or could meet all of our needs. However, the fact is that we are not sheer relationships of love to one another. We remain always and necessarily separate individuals making a *choice* to reach out in love to others. We have our own interests and activities, and are neither willing nor able to be there for one another at every second. Because we exist first as persons in our own right, and then *have* relationships to others, our relationships can come and go. They do not define who we are, nor do they constitute the whole *identity* of our person.

But the divine persons *are* their relations to one another; their relationship to one another defines each person's entire identity and *is* who each one is. They are not first of all persons who then turn toward one another in self-giving. Rather, their *total identity* is to be unreserved givenness: there *is* no Father, Son and Spirit except the three who are complete self-bestowal upon one another. Absolute self-giving is *who* each divine person is, and if they were not total self-communication to one another, they would not be at all.

What are the implications for us? Only a God who is fullness of be-ing can be unbounded self-giving. But as the created offspring of this triune God, we cannot help hungering for a love turned totally toward us and existing absolutely *for* us, because this *is* the kind of love that has given us birth. Each of the divine persons, from whose womb of love we have come, is lavish life by being absolute, unreserved self-giving. Our own inmost call, therefore, is to live this very paradox at the heart of God "If you would gain your life, you must let go of it" (Mk 8:35). To be capable of giving this kind of love is, paradoxically, the fullness of our own identity as unique persons: we become who we are as persons only by growing in communion and relationship with other persons. The more truly distinct and self-possessed we ourselves are, the more generous we are with our persons. Secure in our own identity, we have a surplus of being and love to give to others.

But this kind of love is possible to us only because we ourselves are loved with infinitely gracious gift-love. The whole universe is exploding with the triune God's love, but we ourselves have been made recipients of that effusion as *friends* and, therefore, in some unimaginable way, as equals. The infinite love each divine person has for one another is the same love with which each one of *us* is infinitely loved, and from all eternity. In this boundless triune love we literally "live and move and have our being," becoming more and more who we are meant to be as unique persons. We do not look at ourselves, therefore, and say, "This is what it means to be person; I wonder if God is tri-personal." Rather, it is only in God that the full meaning of personhood lies. Thus, the more we enter into communion with the Three who are the fullness of personhood, the more we ourselves become all that we are meant to be as persons in our own unique richness.

E. CONTEMPORARY CHRISTOLOGICAL AND TRINITARIAN APPROACHES

1. Representative Christological Approaches

Contemporary theologians often combine the kinds of insights of past great Christian thinkers considered in this chapter with modern insights into the meaning of person and community. In this way they attempt to shed new light on the triune God's riches for our own lives today. It is thus helpful for us to have some knowledge of trinitarian reflection of both past and present. And because trinitarian theology is rooted necessarily in christology, we briefly consider first key christological insights of several modern thinkers, and so provide a necessary background for an overview of representative trinitarian approaches of today.

Nicaea had identified Jesus as a divine person in an ontological sense: *who* Jesus is cannot be a *human* (*created*) person, for then he would be simply a bigger and better one of us, able only to be a model for us, but not power within us. Theologians today, however, stress that we come to know Jesus' divinity only in and through his full humanity. It is the *human* life and death of Jesus which unveil to us the God we could never have dared to imagine, the God of absolute self-giving love. Rather than adopting a christology "from above," beginning from the perspective of Jesus' divinity, many theologians today, therefore, approach christology "from below," from the perspective of his full humanity. They thus identify Jesus as a fully human person who is divine.

In addition, contemporary thinkers often emphasize how our own ultimate meaning as human beings is found in Jesus. Wolfhart Pannenberg, for example, stresses that Jesus makes possible the gaining of our full human potential, total dedication to Jesus' Father. In living in unreserved surrender to his Abba, Jesus lives his divine sonship as the "fulfillment of human personality."[8] The more we ourselves learn to hand ourselves over to the Father in our own humanness, the more in this very self-emptying will we gain both the ground and source of our being and our own unique identity and autonomy as human persons.

Especially because of this contemporary emphasis on the relevance of Jesus' humanity for us, contemporary theologians often stress also that conciliar teaching is always formulated in thought categories and terminology that are historically conditioned. They stress, in addition, that Chalcedon is an authoritative beginning, not end, of further insight into the mystery of Jesus' identity as truly human and truly divine. Some of these theologians thus find Chalcedon's identification of Jesus as one divine person with two natures problematic for at least two reasons.[9]

First of all, Chalcedon's definition seems to make humanity and divinity equal categories, as if being human and being divine were simply different ways to live the same kind of existence. These same authors also stress that Chalcedon seems to divide Jesus into a two-level being, yet with the weight so decidedly on the divine that Jesus' true humanity seems secondary. In addition, many people today do not focus on an *ontological* definition of person as a unique, incommunicable subject of a distinct act of existing—that is, as a person who has the human nature common to us all in an *unrepeatable* way. They focus instead on a *psychological* definition of person as a distinct center of self-*consciousness* and freedom. In the past, *nature* was considered the *source* of our human activity and consciousness; today, *person* is considered this source.[10] Contemporary usage in this way describes as "person" what fourth-century thinkers had defined by the term "nature." Some authors, therefore, critique Chalcedon by saying that, given a contemporary understanding of "person," to identify Jesus as the second divine person, pre-existent Word of the Trinity, has no real meaning today.

According to this view, "pre-existent divine person" when applied to Jesus is problematic if not meaningless, since by definition the words cannot refer to Jesus' (created) humanity, and if they refer to Jesus' divinity the effect is to locate "the reality of Jesus very firmly outside the human."[11] Thus, some authors interpret New Testament texts such as John 1:1 about the pre-existent Word who becomes human at the Incarnation and whose name we call Jesus as referring in fact not to the divine Word who is second person of the Trinity but rather to God's *activity* that is personal. In this perspective, Chalcedon's definition is interpreted as applying the term "divine person" to Jesus in a 'highly specialized sense, that is, to capture the unknown content that identifies the divine and human in Jesus."[12]

Unwilling to identify Jesus as the pre-existent Word, second person of the Trinity, some authors thus identify his divinity with his perfect humanity. Piet Schoonenberg, for example, uses a process approach to christology and regards Jesus' humanity as the indispensable vehicle of his divinity: Jesus has become truly divine by being perfectly human.[13] In a similar manner, Jon Sobrino views Jesus as the one who has become liberator of the world through a life-long process, gaining his divine sonship in utter dedication and surrender to his Father. The world's liberation thus requires of us also a like process of growing in our own personal identity as daughters and sons of God; we are to transform the world through our own self-surrender to the God of Jesus.[14] On the other hand, feminist theologians such as Rosemary Radford Ruether[15] and Elisabeth Schüssler Fiorenza[16] emphasize the theme of liberation especially for the women and children of the world oppressed by patriarchal structures. They propose christologies focused on God viewed in Hebrew tradition under the symbol of the feminine figure, *sophia*-wisdom. Jesus is the *sophia*-child of this God, the prophetic liberator of the poor and marginalized who models in his own person, patterns of relating in equality and mutuality.

These and similar contemporary approaches which identify Jesus in terms of his relationship to the first divine person highlight Jesus' life as a process of growing into a perfect humanity equivalent with divinity. While illuminating Jesus' humanity in a way that is meaningful to our own human lives, this kind of approach perhaps does not always do full justice to his divinity, and thus to his deepest significance not simply as model but also as transforming power for us. In a second approach, therefore, Walter Kasper reflects on the person of Jesus in relation not to his Abba, the first divine person, but to the third person, the Holy Spirit. The Spirit who is the very love of God in person so radically fills Jesus that this same Spirit becomes the personal power of love poured out upon the world, uniting us with God and one another precisely through Jesus' resurrection. Jesus thus is not only the bearer but also the giver of the Spirit poured out upon the world to make us a new creation.[17]

In still a third approach, Edward Schillebeeckx responds to theologians who find no meaning in identifying Jesus as God the Word. Schillebeeckx reflects on Jesus' identity precisely as the second person of the Trinity come to human self-consciousness. He finds the idea proposed by some contemporary theologians that Jesus is not the pre-existent Word—and therefore that God is not eternally triune but becomes trinitarian only at the Incarnation—"inconceivable." Like that of Kasper, Rahner, and William Hill, whose insights we consider below, his own approach is consistent with Chalcedon's intent to guard the reality of Jesus as divine, saving power for us, and articulates our own approach in this book. In his focus on the central event of Jesus' resurrection, Schillebeeckx stresses in effect that Jesus is a human person in the contemporary psychological sense, but is also the second divine person in the ontological sense: "The man Jesus . . . is identically the Son . . . the 'Second Person' of the Trinitarian plenitude of divine unity." In other words, who he is is the second person of the triune God, not only human model but also true saving power for us, offering us through his resurrection forgiveness and a whole new way to live our lives as human beings.[18]

While Leontius of Byzantium and Thomas Aquinas had explained that the human *nature* of Jesus is enhypostatic, that is, exists, in the divine person of the Son, Schillebeeckx emphasizes that Jesus is a truly human *person* in the psychological sense, "enhypostatic" in the divine person of God the Son and Word. In this way, the incarnation shows us a God who, in a way we could never have imagined, is "*Deus humanissimus,*" "God most human." But the mystery of how the man Jesus can be truly the second person of the triune God is so gracious and unfathomable a mystery that it leads us finally "to be silent and to adore."[19]

Karl Rahner, too, focuses on the identity of the Word as second person of the triune God. He adopts a "transcendental christology" and considers the conditions within us which transcend all particular historical circumstances and which cry out for and presuppose the answer to the question we are as human beings. In this way he illumines how Jesus is the fulfillment of all our human longings, the unrepeatable meeting point and culmination of God's absolute self-giving and the evolutionary process of the cosmos toward transcendence. Just as the Word is the perfect self-expression of the Father within God, the humanity of Jesus in turn is the created self-expression of the Word outside of God. Because we ourselves exist as human beings in order to receive this Word's self-communication in absolute love, our own humanity thus finds its ultimate and exalted meaning as the very created self-expression of God the Word.[20]

2. Representative Trinitarian Approaches

This overview of christological approaches leads us to consider briefly some representative ways of thinking about the Trinity today. For this purpose, William Hill's summary of key contemporary approaches to trinitarian theology is of particular value to us.

For some thinkers, the Trinity is less the living God than an idea, a doctrine that is helpful though not essential to our Christian faith. Theologians such as Friedrich Schleiermacher,

Paul Tillich, and Cyril Richardson view the Trinity as a *symbol*, not for who God really is, but for our own *ideas* about God. Thus, the Trinity is not God but rather a *concept* or *idea* of God.[21] In contrast, theologians such as Karl Barth and Karl Rahner identify the Trinity as the living God, and thus, as the very center of our Christian faith. But they caution against a tritheism which could result from applying the modern psychological understanding of "person" to God. They therefore adopt a "neo-modal" approach, focusing on the unity of God and viewing the Trinity as three modes of being, modes of God's self-revelation (Barth), or manners of subsisting (Rahner).[22]

Rahner in particular finds a helpful illumination of the triune God's identity in reflecting on the transcendent God's (the Father's) self-communications as Word and Spirit. The Father is the eternally self-expressive God, and the Word is this God's absolute self-giving as gift and promise in history. When God gives, however, the gift is not simply something God has, for all that God has, God *is*. When God gives, therefore, the gift is nothing less than the very *self* of God—the Word. Further, the very power to *receive* this gift *is* God—the Spirit. The Father thus has two self-communications, the Word and the Spirit. The Word is the Father's self-communication in Jesus as *promise* and *gift* in our *history*. The Spirit, on the other hand, is the divine person who is the very power within us to *accept* this gift. The Spirit in this way is the Father's self-communication as *transcendent fulfillment* that will be achieved in its completion in the *future*.[23]

Other theologians view the Trinity in "neo-economic" terms, centering on the God we know through the divine activity in history. Some process theologians view God as the dynamism of process and becoming, a God who becomes "di-polar" rather than triune, a God of transcendence ("the Father") and of closeness and immanence (Jesus).[24] In this di-polar approach, the Spirit often is considered an impersonal creative force of God ("the Father") or the impersonal force of Jesus' presence to us today.

On the other hand, thinkers such as Piet Schoonenberg stress that we should say about God only what we can see and experience in Jesus and his history. Because speaking about a pre-existent Word seems problematic in this context, his approach focuses on the divine Word which begins to exist when Jesus comes into being; God becomes Trinity in history.[25] In this historical approach, some thinkers also emphasize the identity of God as the dynamism of an *event* rather than as the static nature of a "being." Jürgen Moltmann thus views the Trinity as the "event of the cross," the event of love that comes into being when the Spirit of love is born of the Father's and Son's mutual suffering at Calvary.[26]

Finally, although little has been written explicitly about the Trinity from a feminist perspective, the roots of a feminist interpretation of trinitarian doctrine can be found, for example, in the christological approaches of theologians such as Rosemary Radford Ruether[27] and Elisabeth Schüssler Fiorenza.[28] In his own christology, William Thompson argues that in light of the male images and names for the triune God which now predominate in our prayer and talk, we need a "feminist revision of our Trinitarian symbolism too, if this is to remain a viable symbol for all. Father, Son, and Spirit needs complementing and correcting by Mother, Daughter, and Love."[29] Some contemporary theologians point out that our mystical tradition does provide us with feminine images for God. As we have seen, Julian of Norwich writes of "our Mother Jesus,"[30] and Catherine of Siena speaks of the Holy Spirit as our mother who nurses us at the breast of God.[31] Mechtilde of Magdeburg also refers to the triune God in feminine images: "The Trinity is like a mother's cloak wherein the child finds a home and lays its head on the maternal breast."[32]

Following the insight of Ruether, however, theologians such as William Thompson caution also that attempting a feminist interpretation of trinitarian doctrine will not be helpful if it simply names one or more of the divine persons "she," or relies simply on "androgynous" christologies which view Jesus as the feminine wisdom of God personified. This kind of approach only furthers the equation of "femaleness with the supposed feminine qualities of nurturing" and thus fails to promote the true liberation of women and men, both of whom are called to tenderness as well as to strength, to service as well as to full realization of their creative potential.[33]

The above mentioned approaches focus on the divine oneness in ways that do not always illumine the triune distinction in God. Other theologians, in contrast, center on the Three who are God rather than on God's unity. The medieval theologian Richard of St. Victor (*De Trinitate* III) had reflected on the triune God through meditating on our experience as distinct human persons loving one another. Love is a union between two persons who cherish one another's good. But love reaches its fullness only in a third person mutually beloved by both. The presence of a third thus lifts their love out of a narrow preoccupation with each other into the fullest realization of love as altruistic self-giving. The perfection of love in this way overflows outward in an unbounded movement of expansiveness.

It is this insight which underlies the "societal" model of trinitarian reflection. One human analogue used in this understanding is the very structure of the human family. We see this remarkable sign of our trinitarian origin in the husband and wife whose love overflows the boundaries of simply their own union and bears fruit in the child of their love. An exquisite suggestion of the Trinity whose love ultimately has given each one of us birth is thus etched into the very heart of our existence as human persons. Because we come into being only as the child of a father and mother, our most basic societal unit is itself trinitarian. This very structure of our family life is a pale reflection of the infinitely lavish love at the heart of the Trinity, the eternal activity of loving between Father and Son which bears fruit in the very person of the Spirit.

Contemporary thinkers such as Joseph Bracken have found helpful insights in this societal model of trinitarian understanding, although in an earlier work he envisages the Trinity as having three consciousnesses and thus approaches a tritheistic understanding.[34] Other theologians such as Eberhart Jüngel[35] and Heribert Mühlen consider the triune personality of God through reflecting on the model of human *speech* in its *relational* nature. Mühlen in particular focuses on the phenomenology of our consciousness: we communicate in an interpersonal interaction dynamically structured as "I—Thou—We." The Spirit thus can be seen as the very communion, the living person who is the "We" of the "I" of the Father and the "Thou" of the Son.[36]

William Hill[37] also presents in his trinitarian theology an illumination of the unique identity of each person. The triune God is not a static "being" but sheer dynamism—not of continual becoming but of infinite actuality and plenitude of Being. And if we complement our modern psychological understanding of "person" as a distinct center of consciousness with an ontological understanding of person as a distinct, incommunicable subject, we illumine the meaning of the Trinity precisely as tri-personal. The triune God thus does not mean three separate consciousnesses, but three distinct centers and subjects of one same divine conscious life. The triune God is not three gods, but one *same* life and truth and goodness itself, yet as three who are infinitely, uniquely "person" in a way that utterly transcends all we could imagine.

This dynamic life of the triune God overflows in the infinite expansive activities of unbounded knowing and loving: the Father is the knowing one; the Son, the Word infinitely known and said. The Spirit is the very *koinonia* or dynamic *communion* of love between Father and Son as Knower and Word known. Thus the triune God is infinitely *relational*: self-expressive in knowing and self-unitive in loving.

In a complementary insight, Walter Kasper stresses that the Spirit as love and communion in God is also the utter "ecstasy" of God directed outward. The overflowing abundance of the triune God's inner life bursting infinitely outward is the surprise of absolutely gracious love and beauty and new life poured out among us in the very person of the Spirit. The Spirit in this way is the unbounded freedom of the triune God's inner love gratuitously lavished on us and permeating the entire universe.[38]

The very plentitude of God as the mystery of utter unity and yet sheer distinction, and the relevance of this divine mystery for our own meaning, are thus a common focus of contemporary trinitarian theology. There is no union in the cosmos that can be anything but a hint and taste of the unspeakable oneness of the three divine persons. Yet the divine persons are not clones of one another; no one is more fully and uniquely person than each of the divine persons. And wherever we also see great diversity of personality among us, we see a pale shadow of the fullness of personhood in its diversity and incommunicable distinction within the triune God. Our human race itself, created distinctly and indivisible as woman and man, reflects our trinitarian origin in a God who is irreducible distinction at the heart of absolute unity.

All of our own union and personal uniquenesses thus stem only from the womb of this tri-personal God. This is why when we enter into relationship with the Three who are God, we not only grow in union among us, but also gain who we are as an unrepeatably unique person created in the image of the triune God's abundant richness. In this way, the Trinity is unveiled as the definitive meaning of the entire universe, for in the triune God alone do we find the source, ground, and goal of the whole cosmos, the mystery of lavish personal distinction in the paradox of utter union of life.

4

Knowing the Triune God

In the last two chapters we have considered the meaning of Jesus' paschal mystery and some of the Christian community's most significant efforts to speak about the triune God who draws us into this mystery in our own lives. We turn now to reflect on what the paschal event unveils to us about the very heart of the triune God, about the alluring depths of each divine person's unique identity. The three divine persons are inseparably one same God, and yet, as we keep this most fundamental truth of our faith always before our eyes, we shall see in this chapter how the cross and resurrection illumine in a special way the inmost identity of the Father, as well as the inner mystery of Jesus' person as radiant Word and icon of his Abba. Pentecost, the glorious culmination of the paschal event, in turn unveils the very secret at the heart of the triune God, the brilliant transparency of the Holy Spirit.

A. PRELIMINARY CONSIDERATION

1. Knowing the Divine Persons

As we begin our reflections, we draw attention to three presuppositions which underlie the insights of this chapter. We need to ask, first of all, whether it really matters if we know the divine persons distinctly. Isn't it enough simply to realize that there *is* a triune God, and to experience the *activity* of this God among us?

To answer this question, it is helpful to reflect on a basic human need we have, the need to give and receive from one another not simply objects which signify our love but the most precious of gifts, our*selves*. This is why we are not satisfied with simply knowing our loved ones' outward actions, or observing their beauty from afar. On the contrary, we desire to share in their inmost heart and soul, to participate in the very secret and mystery of their being. And yet, because our lives are often opaque rather than transparent, perhaps few of us ever achieve this kind of union with another. We mask rather than unveil who we really are, and protect ourselves by closing ourselves and shutting others out. Nevertheless, even as we resist one another, what we most *want* is to be known, and to know not only the external actions but also the inner depths of those we love.

Because the most alluring of the triune God's creation is still the inexhaustible mystery we call "person," in the end, we cannot help desiring to touch and to share in the "always more" at the heart of our loved ones in their own uniqueness. And whenever through God's grace we do choose to become vulnerable, we bestow on one another nothing less than the gift of ourselves in our irreplaceable personhood. This is all the more true when we speak of the infinite and inexhaustible persons who are God. What we experience of the Trinity's presence and activity among us cannot help making us thirst for the very mystery of the triune God's own inner life and beauty, the mysterious depths of each divine person's infinite uniqueness.

We confess our faith in this God by using in the creed the magnificient symbol of light—a symbol which hints at how unreservedly the divine persons bathe us in the gift of themselves. We realize that in the night we see only darkness, but when sunlight wakens the world, everything around us seems to burst open with unreserved transparency to us. Nothing seems held back from us; everything seems to glow with warmth, beckoning us to enter into its beauty, to share in its inner secret. In the same way, for those who have the eyes to see, the triune God's activity in us and in the entire universe radiates with infinite transparency. The depths of the triune God's own inner life literally permeate our entire cosmos and flow outward to us in a ceaseless self-giving that truly unveils and gives to us the very heart of God. Thus, the trinitarian life is not lived above and beyond us in a far away heaven closed off to us. Rather, what the triune God does for us is also who the triune God really is, not simply for us but in the infinite ocean of love that is the divine life.

Even more, saints and mystics like Catherine of Siena, Julian of Norwich, Ignatius of Loyola and John of the Cross have realized that the desire to know the divine persons more deeply, far from being tritheism, takes us to the very heart of our Christian faith. For the triune God is not one as a solitary individual with simply three different names but as a God in whose depths there is truly a threefold distinction. And just as we come to know other persons only by taking the risk of becoming vulnerable and opening ourselves to conscious communion with them, so too, we allow the divine persons to make their impact of love on us by entering into communion with them precisely in the vast mystery of their own unique identities. In this chapter, therefore, we seek to know the triune God in the biblical sense, not simply by studying ideas but also by opening our minds and hearts to recognize in our own experience the unspeakably lovely depths of each divine person's unique identity.

2. Grace and the Missions

Our second presupposition assumes that the very possibility of "knowing" the divine persons in the biblical sense is the result only of the undeserved gift of grace to us. It is true that all that we are and have is gift; we ourselves and all of creation exist only because of the infinite largesse of the triune God. But beyond the free bounty bestowed on us in our own existence and that of the world around us, we need to distinguish the infinitely more gratuitous realm of "grace." The triune God's self-disclosure to us is a *self-communication* through a created participation in the divine life itself. This very gift draws us as persons capable of knowing and loving into the inmost life of the triune God, into mutuality and friendship with the very Three who are God.

Even in our own relationships with one another we cannot

help experiencing a faithful, unreserved, and mutual vulnerability as absolutely undeserved gift. Yet revealing our deepest secrets, our inmost being to another, demands of us such unconditional trust and vulnerability that many of us do not ever share ourselves in this most intimate way with anyone, not even with our beloved spouse or friend. And even if we were willing to open ourselves completely to another, many of us have never found another person who seemed trustworthy enough to receive and treasure the gift of our self-revelation.

All the more, then, the triune God's unreserved self-disclosure to us of the divine life as *triune* is a self-giving not only of the most intimate but also of the most undeserved and unexpected kind. We are not equals but only creatures of this God, human persons who are weak and fallible and often faithless. Nevertheless, what we have received in the incarnation of the Word and the outpouring of the Spirit far exceeds the gift even of our created existence. In these two missions or sendings the very *uncreated grace* or gift of the divine persons themselves—the Word and Spirit, and with them, the Father who sends them— intimately offer themselves to us. In and through the gift of created grace we participate in these two missions and attain to intimate communion with the divine persons in their own uniqueness.

3. Appropriation

This last point brings us to our third presupposition. Our communion with the Trinity is one which we can wordlessly experience. But since the mystery of "person," and far more, of "divine person," infinitely exceeds all that our concepts and words could grasp, how can we possibly begin to *articulate* the mystery of the divine persons in their own unique identities? It is here, at this point, that we can use a way of speaking about the triune God called "appropriation"—designating one particular divine person through an activity or attribute that is in fact common to all three. In so using this form of paradox we can give an *intimation* of one of the persons with whom that activity or attribute bears a specific *affinity*. For example, because the activity of creating bears a particular likeness to the identity of the first person as ultimate source, we often name the Father also as "Creator." In fact, however, all three divine persons have created us. The three are one same God, and, therefore, all that the persons do outside the inner divine life—except for the missions of the Word in the paschal mystery of Jesus and of the Spirit in the mystery of pentecost—is the one same activity of the one same God.

Yet the divine persons are *distinct* in their unique personhood because of their relationships to one another within the depths of the divine life—relationships that are *ordered* but not subordinated to one another. Thus, only the Abba of Jesus is the "first" divine person; only Jesus is the "second" person, and the Spirit alone is the "third" person. Each divine person, therefore, also creates *uniquely*. Only the first divine person creates as ultimate source and origin; only the Word creates as exemplar in whose image all else is made; and only the Spirit creates as the goal for which we are made—participation in the very love at the heart of the triune God.

Appropriation in this way functions as symbolic language which not only suggests the identity of each person but also and ultimately leads us to personal *encounter* with the three in their own uniqueness. This intimate encounter is possible because the Trinity is present not only within all of creation as its maker and goal, but also through grace within us as the God whom we can encounter personally through our knowing and loving. Even more, each divine person is present within us in a way that is not appropriated but uniquely *proper* to that person.

Thus, for example, all three of the divine persons intimately dwell within us, making their home in us and our home in them. But because the Spirit is the personal bond of love uniting Father and Son, this same Spirit is the one who joins us to the inner divine life; the Holy Spirit is the very person of our union with the triune God. Just as every gift proceeds *to us* in the Spirit, through Jesus, from his Abba, first divine person, so, too, we return *to our Abba* by the preeminent dwelling in us of the Holy Spirit, third person at the very heart of God. In a unique way, then, the Spirit, the very term of the Father and Son's mutual loving, is *the* uncreated gift of love dwelling intimately within us and whose very *presence* unites us with Jesus, and through him, to his Abba.[1]

Having briefly considered the importance of our knowing

the persons in their unique identities, the gift of grace as the source for this kind of knowing, and the purpose of appropriation as a way to speak about the Trinity, we turn now to reflect in further detail on the identities of the Three who are God. In this chapter we consider how, in a self-revelation unreserved in its vulnerability and trust, the divine persons offer to us through the paschal event the infinite treasure of their own unique identities.

B. THE CROSS AND RESURRECTION OF JESUS AND THE PERSONAL IDENTITY OF HIS ABBA

Having already considered in chapter one the mystery of the Father and in chapters two and three the mystery of Jesus, we reflect here only briefly on how the cross and resurrection especially illumine the depths of each in their unique personhood.

The disciples could not know at first that the inmost mystery of the God whom Jesus called "Abba" would be unveiled to them only in a paradox, at once the most terrible and most beautiful drama the world would ever witness. They could not know that calling God "Abba" as Jesus had taught them would take him and them to the cross, and that here alone the inmost heart of this God would be definitively unveiled. At the cross, they had to watch what they could not believe: Jesus, beloved of his Abba, lies absolutely abandoned. "He trusts in God; let God deliver him now, if he desires him; for he said, 'I am the Son of God'" (MT 27:43). No one answers Jesus' terrified cries, "My God, my God, why hast thou forsaken me" (Mt - 27:46).

There is no escape for Jesus, beloved of God. The torments of doubt and fear shatter his mind and heart as cruelly as the nails rip open his flesh. And yet in the very midst of this terror, something extraordinary happens. In the torments of his final agony, suffocated by the doubt and sheer void that closes him off from his Abba, Jesus makes one last unreserved act of self-giving; he throws himself into death's hideous pit and cries out to its emptiness, "Abba." In the same breath, his lips utter the astounding words full of healing, "Forgive them" (Lk - 23:34).

And then the infinite paradox is revealed: "The one who sees me, sees the Father" (Jn 14:8). On the cross, the face of the transcendent God of the universe is unveiled as the absolute antithesis, the complete reversal of all that our human ideas would expect or imagine. The God who is origin of all is not the domineering ruler of the universe, but the God of Jesus, the God who forgives and heals us by entering with us into the very depths of our weakness. This is the God of tender-hearted mercy and compassion, of life more powerful than any death, of love stronger than any sin. Having thrown himself into the pit of cruelty and abandonment and death, Jesus finds himself in the arms of the God of compassion and mercy and life. At the heart of hatred and betrayal, in the pit of death itself, the face of Jesus' Abba is unveiled. This is the God of unconquerable life, of unquenchable love, of unconditional forgiveness so vast that in its embrace the torments of death itself turn into lavish, unbounded life.

Divine paradox which the human heart could never guess: the inmost identity of the first divine person is not the force of manipulation and oppression but the power of unrestrained love. The cross itself discloses the posture of our Abba toward us: like a table spread open and defenseless, the God of infinite tenderness waits for us, offering us as a banquet in Jesus nothing less than the very flesh of God.[2] The final word of the entire universe and of our own personal existence is life, not death; love, not revenge. Jesus' Abba is the beginning and end, the ultimate source and final fulfillment of all that is, reigning over the cosmos not with oppressive force but with love infinitely tender and strong.

Jesus' Abba is in truth Yahweh, transcendent God of the universe worshipped by the Jews. But the very word which defines the unspeakable name of Yahweh, "hesed," connotes compassion, tenderness, and pity because it comes from the root word for "womb." Is 42:14 and Deut 32:18 depict this same God as a mother in labor, while Is 66:9-13 portrays God as birthing us from an open womb, nursing and comforting us on the divine breast. The author of Psalm 131 speaks of resting confidently in God the way a quieted child sleeps at his or her mother's breast.

The Abba of Jesus is thus also true mother to us, yearning

over her children, feeding them at her breast, and caring for every single one. The God of Jesus bears us within the divine womb of love the way a mother carries her child within her, bears us in his arms the way a father protects his child. Because of this, each one of us has a name, a source, a purpose and meaning, a home. Only in the arms of this Abba do we find who we really are: "You are no longer strangers and aliens or foreigners. No, you are members of the household of God" (Eph 2:19). In the heart of our Father we hear the words which speak the entire identity of Jesus, and which now in Jesus define the identity of each one of us: "You are my beloved daughter, my beloved son."

To call God "Abba" in the sense in which Jesus bids us to do so is thus not to give God a title. Rather, it is to enter into the very heart of God, magnificent source of all that is, creator of the galaxies of heaven and the depths of the ocean, and to find here my own ultimate origin and identity. In this heart I hear the call of my own unique name and surrender myself to the flood tide of love and mercy in the one who is *my* source and final goal. In the arms of my Abba, I find my beginning and end, my name and identity, my family roots and heritage, my own personal meaning and irreplaceable reason for existing. In these arms my inmost desire to know from where I have come and where I am going finds its ultimate answer. In the infinitely loving, powerful, and protective embrace of this Abba I myself in all that I am, as well as the entire universe with all of its splendor, find our true home.

C. THE CROSS AND RESURRECTION AND THE PERSONAL IDENTITY OF JESUS

The cross unveiling the face of Jesus' Abba was not the final word. The crucifixion itself ends in an outcome that our wildest dreams could not have imagined: not simply a resuscitation doomed to another eventual death, but a glorious resurrection that radically transforms the destiny of the whole cosmos. The infinite love pent up within Jesus is finally unleashed in its full force in the unspeakable act of love which is his death. The Spirit of love contained by the human body of Jesus before his death bursts now through even the bonds of his body. The Spirit so permeates his body that it becomes absolutely radiant with unbounded beauty and eschatological glory, until his flesh itself utterly transcends the limits of time and space.

This, finally, is the mystery of Jesus' resurrection. His risen body is not opaque but absolutely transparent; it does not hide but actually *gives* who he is. Our own bodies now often mask our true identity and prevent us from being in true contact and relationship with one another, but Jesus' human destiny, his glorious resurrection, has now become our own in him. Because of Jesus, heaven will be joined to earth in our very bodies. At our own resurrection, we will be transparent and vulnerable to one another not in spite of the created matter of our radiant risen bodies but rather *through* them. Our Spirit-permeated bodies will be the very transparency of our persons and will no longer hide who we truly are but rather reveal and give it. Instead of being opaque and closed, holding ourselves back from one another, our human bodies in their risen glory will bestow our inmost mystery on one another. This richness of our mutual self-donation will thus share in the very mystery of the triune God's infinite, interpersonal self-giving.

The eschatological splendor of Jesus' resurrection in this way finally reveals his own inmost identity: "He is the image of the invisible God . . . all things were created through him and for him. . . . In him all the fulness of God was pleased to dwell, and through him to reconcile to himself all things . . . making peace by the blood of the cross" (Col 1:15-16, 19-20). Paradoxically, the God whose flesh has reconciled heaven with earth is revealed in his glorious resurrection as absolute self-surrender, infinitely humble self-giving. Drawing all that he is from his Abba, Jesus discloses his very *identity* as absolute receptivity, sheer self-surrender, unreserved, unending *yes* to his Abba: "All that is mine is yours" (Jn 17:10). Even more, the paradox revealed in Jesus breaks forth in his resurrection to become in a created way our paradox also. As we grow more surrendered and receptive, more unreserved in our self-giving to our Abba, we become more fully who we are meant to be. Yet we gain who we are only by giving who we are and thus by participating in the same mystery at the heart of God.

Jesus, second divine person, perfect image and self-expression of his Abba, joins heaven and earth and all of the created cosmos in his risen body. In his humanity, everything material and created is full of value, every human person is of irreplaceable worth. In him and through the force of his love, everything has meaning; everything—even our weakness and sin—finds its healing. Mystics such as Julian of Norwich picture us enclosed in Jesus as in the womb of our true mother. In our sin we can run with absolute confidence to these arms of grace and mercy.[3] They are not the arms of a God "unable to sympathize with our weakness," but one whom love has driven to share our human lot in every way, one who "in every respect has been tempted as we are, yet without sinning" (Heb 4:15). As a mother gives her child to drink of her own milk, our "Precious mother Jesus" gives us his own flesh and "the precious plenty" of his blood to feed us with life itself and nurture us unto our own resurrection.[4]

In the arms of this our brother stretched out upon the cross we find not only understanding and forgiveness, but also the power of the resurrection to free and transform us from within, making us an absolutely new creation. The resurrection of Jesus swallows up in victory that last enemy of the human race that alone could finally destroy us, death itself. The whole material cosmos thus finds its destiny in Jesus' glorious resurrection: "O death, where is thy victory? O death, where is thy sting?" (1 Cor 15:54-55). In the resurrection of Jesus, death is conquered; life, unending, unquenchable life reigns!

D. PENTECOST AND THE PERSONAL IDENTITY OF THE HOLY SPIRIT

1. The Mystery of Pentecost

Jesus' resurrection unveils his inmost identity as Word of God, perfect icon of the Father, in whose human, Spirit-permeated flesh death itself has been vanquished. Yet even Jesus' glorious resurrection was not the final word of the triune God's heart to us. Pentecost, the outpouring of the Spirit who is "Giver of life," alone culminates and brings to its full and glorious completion the paschal mystery. Before Jesus' death, the Holy Spirit, the very love between Jesus and his Father, filled and permeated his entire being; his unreserved self-giving to his Abba is the total content of Jesus' identity. Yet before his death, this Spirit of love was confined, so to speak, by the opaque boundaries of Jesus' human existence. His pre-risen body could only "contain" rather than itself convey the Spirit.

But at his crucifixion, Jesus' infinite love for his Abba and for all of the world gathered into one great impulse and torrent until even the finite bounds of his human body could not resist its force. Like a tremendous wave shattering the walls that have held it back, the flood of love in Jesus' heart would not be contained. "Father, forgive them. . . . Father, into thy hands I commend my spirit" (Lk 23:34, 36). In the very outpouring of his life in death, the force of the Spirit's love filling Jesus' entire identity bursts forth even through the bonds of his human existence. The Spirit's love so permeates and transforms his broken and lifeless body that in this human body he now becomes not simply alive again but *"life-giving spirit"* (1 Cor 15:45).

This is why, far from being simply an attractive epilogue to the death and resurrection of Jesus, a lovely addendum to the paschal mystery, pentecost is its very completion and goal. For the Holy Spirit *is* the power of love and unconquerable life which burst the bonds of death at Jesus' resurrection. "Hope does not disappoint us, because God's love has been poured into our hearts through the Holy Spirit who has been given to us" (Rom 5:5). Jesus' entire purpose among us, therefore, is to bring us to pentecost, to give us the Holy Spirit.[5]

Filled with the Spirit's peace and courage, with the certainty of being loved and forgiven, the early Christians preached the power of Jesus' resurrection and offered this new life to others. This same Spirit of love began so transforming their hearers that the early community could see in this outpouring nothing less than the fulfillment of the end time promised by Joel. "In the last days it shall be, God declares, that I will pour out my Spirit upon all flesh, and your sons and your daughters shall prophesy" (Acts 2:17).

The Spirit of love who had anointed Jesus (Acts 10:38) now possessed the disciples of Jesus and turned the Jewish Christians' deepest sensitivities upside down. Luke tells of Peter's encounter with the pagan Cornelius and the Holy Spirit's utter reversal of all Peter had held dear. "You yourselves know how unlawful it is for a Jew to associate with or visit anyone of another nation; but God has shown me that I should not call anyone common or unclean"(Acts 10:28). The Jewish believers who would have nothing to do with pagan Gentiles had to submit all they would have planned to the unexpected surprises of the Holy Spirit. While Peter was still speaking, "the Holy Spirit fell on all who heard the word. And the believers from among the circumcised who came with Peter were amazed, because the gift of the Holy Spirit had been poured out even on the Gentiles. For they heard them speaking in tongues and extolling God"(Acts 10:45-46).

This lavish, startling gift of the Spirit among them brought Jewish and Gentile Christians a freedom they could not have imagined. Their hearts were opened to love, their tongues unloosed to praise. Luke depicts the Jerusalem community as filled with the self-giving love of Jesus' own heart. "The company of those who believed were of one heart and soul . . . they had everything in common . . . and great grace was upon them all. There was not a needy person among them, for . . . distribution was made to each as any had need" (Acts 4:32, 34). The unique gifts of each person began to flourish under the warmth and light of the Spirit's and community's care: "There are varieties of gifts but the same Spirit . . . to each is given the manifestation of the Spirit for the common good" (1 Cor 12:4, 7).

2. Gift of Love Poured Out Upon the World

The mystery of this Spirit who as subsistent love itself has no human "face" is the most elusive of the divine persons. Scriptural authors and other writers throughout the ages have used images and symbols to convey something of the Spirit's beautiful and powerful personality: the lightness and grace of a bird, the warmth and force of fire; the cooling, life-giving refreshment of water. Luke identifies the Holy Spirit as the whole treasure of God's heart (Lk 11:13; Acts 2:38). After the Holy Spirit's outpouring upon us through the risen flesh of Jesus, there is literally nothing more to give us. In the Holy Spirit we receive the very person of infinite love between Father and Son. The Spirit is their embrace, their kiss, their joy and delight lavished upon the world.

The Holy Spirit is the sword of truth, the ecstasy and power of God, raging like a storm and flood and driving wind, uncontrollable, unpredictable. The Spirit is like a gentle breeze on a hot day, or the aroma of an exquisite perfume; like the loveliness of a haunting melody or the fresh bright newness of a spring day bathed in sunlight. Yet the Spirit of the living God is none of these created things. Every image can only hint at the Spirit's depths as third divine person: powerfully and gently present among and within us as the very heart of God, bestowed upon us as the completion which all of the symbols promise, given now as the pledge of our final possession (2 Cor 5:5), and, at the end, lavished upon us as our last and infinitely extravagant fulfillment.

The third divine person's name as Spirit itself connotes the breath and sigh of infinite love between Jesus and his Abba. Because love is the very source and cause of every other gift we bestow, the spirit's name is not only "Love" but also "Gift." "You shall receive the gift of the Holy Spirit" (Acts 2:38). But this gift is offered to us so that it may truly be ours in an unreturnable bestowal. Thus the Holy Spirit is not only our Abba's Spirit, not only Jesus' Spirit, but truly *our* Spirit as well, given not only to bring us created gifts of healing and love but also the very uncreated gift of the Spirit's own intimate friendship to enjoy.[6] In this way the Holy Spirit is the "innermost" heart of the triune God bestowed on us through Jesus' resurrection as the "outermost" extension of God's heart.[7] We enter into the triune life through this Spirit, third divine person, because the Spirit comes to make us vulnerable to love, to make our hearts big enough to embrace the entire world with the very love at the heart of the triune God.

Wherever we find a true love story, therefore, we find also the Spirit of the living God. Our human destiny is not that of isolated egos turned inward but rather of autonomous persons so inwardly secure that we freely turn outward to communion with others. As the very person of love at the heart of God, the Spirit gently and strongly attracts us, healing our wounded wills and freeing us for generous self-giving. Mystics such as Catherine of Siena have so experienced the Spirit filling their hearts that they have seen in the Holy Spirit our mother, nursing us with the infinite gift-love at the heart of God.[8] And this gift-love, *agape*, is not simply the effect of the Spirit's work in us but mysteriously a created participation in the very person of the Holy Spirit.[9]

Whenever the Holy Spirit is truly present, this same Spirit always binds us more closely to our brothers and sisters, especially those most unloved and in need. This is why mystics have often seen the inseparable connection between the Holy Spirit's fire of love and the eucharist, in which Jesus' unreserved gift-love joins us both to God and to one another. The Spirit who is the personal bond of love at the heart of God thus draws us into community and, in a miracle of grace that only the Spirit can effect, makes us one in our very uniqueness and diversity.

3. Experiencing the Holy Spirit

The Holy Spirit is the "joyous possession" we read about in the Scriptures, the one who transformed the lives of the early Christians, filling them with joy and peace and unselfish love. Yet where can we ourselves find the Holy Spirit in our lives and world today? We often expect to find the Spirit only outside of us, in "spiritual" places. But the Holy Spirit, inmost heart of God, will be found rather in our inmost being and experience. When we ache for love, for inner peace, for contentment of mind and heart, whether we realize it or not, we ache in fact for the Holy Spirit, the Spirit who gives freedom and confidence and joy. The Holy Spirit is the anonymous person hidden in the depths of our every-day experience. When we break out of the prison of our egoism in a way that surprises even us, when we taste true joy and not simply pleasure, when we do not run away from our loneliness, when we accept and embrace without cynicism the "fragmentary experiences" of love and beauty and joy . . . here is the Spirit of God.[10]

When we dare "to pray into a silent darkness" and trust that we are heard; when we open ourselves to relationship with another, truly giving of ourselves rather than merely taking; when we are drawn by a power setting us on a course we would not have planned for ourselves; when we encounter the uncontrollable and undefinable power of love in our lives, we are in the presence of the Spirit of God. *This* is the "mysticism of every day life, the discovery of God in everything, the sober intoxication of the Spirit."[11] By entering more fully and deeply into ourselves, into the joys and sorrows of our own lives and those of the whole world, we discover the Holy Spirit as our inmost depths. This is what it means to be a mystic, not primarily one who enjoys extraordinary experiences, visions and revelations, but rather a person who lives enveloped by the love of the triune God.

By our very immersion into the Christian community through the sacraments of initiation, this treasure is meant for and available to each one of us. Yet while the Spirit of God wants to draw us completely into the incomprehensible love at the heart of God, we often want the Holy Spirit only in small doses. We fear the incalculable surprises of the Spirit, and fear giving up the control we suppose we exercise over our own lives. We are afraid to believe that God could really love us, afraid to yield ourselves into the arms of love.

Yet to this Spirit who is God's "innermost mystery," we are called to deliver ourselves as to *our* innermost mystery. Once we taste the Holy Spirit in our own lives, we begin to take the Holy Spirit we have received in baptism seriously. We no longer consider the Holy Spirit simply as the seasoning of another's existence, but as the "incomprehensible ground, the innermost center" in which our own life finds its meaning.[12]

The Holy Spirit is the very light of love and peace itself permeating our lives even in their darkness and pain. We may have experienced flying in a plane on a dismal day only to find ourselves suddenly far above the clouds where the sun is shining brilliantly. Our own lives are often filled with what seems to be only disappointment and tragedy. Yet if in prayer we looked more deeply we could find hidden even in our suffering the light and power of the Spirit. We could discover radiance transfiguring our darkness, softening what has become hard and dry in us, breaking down our barriers and resistance, refreshing our hearts with the peace only God can give.

The Spirit's love is meant to permeate our entire being with light powerful enough to transfigure not only our hearts but also our faces as well. The story is told of an eastern mystic, Seraphim of Sarov, whose face often was brilliant with light. The saint once encountered a disciple who, on seeing Seraphim's shining face, wanted to know how he, too, could find the Holy Spirit in his own life. Seraphim prayed that the young man would realize, that because of his baptism, this same resplendent light of the Spirit enfolded him also. As Seraphim prayed, the disciple began to be aware of a sense of infinite calm and well-being deep within him, the peace of the Holy Spirit promised to each one of us: "My peace I give to you" (Jn 14:27).[13]

Yet the Spirit is not only light for us but also life itself, life that comes from breathing air so infinitely fresh and delicate that we do not know its origin or where it will lead us (Jn 3:8). Each one of us has experienced in some way these gentle and unpredictable movements of the Holy Spirit which open us to deeper love, leading us where we would not have planned to go and yet where we could resist going only at the price of our own identity. The Holy Spirit thus invites us to an unreserved surrender and self-giving that will well up within us as a continual, wordless prayer, "Spirit of love, make me docile to your most gentle leadings."

Drawing us *"fortiter et suaviter"*—strongly and gently—the Spirit in this way works in us with both power and might, but also with sweetness, with tenderness. Often, it is only long after a significant event in our lives that we recognize the Holy Spirit's hidden, tender, and powerful presence. Far from being a controlling and manipulating force outside us, the Spirit is the very person of love at the heart of God who gently and strongly lays hold of our own inmost freedom through love.[14] The radical paradox, therefore, is that the entire task and goal of our life is to allow ourselves to be overcome and possessed, as it were, by this Holy Spirit of love. Our every work is meant to deliver us into the vast embrace of the Spirit at the heart not only of the triune God but also of our inmost being as well.

E. THE TRIUNE GOD, OUR HOME

Julian of Norwich writes with particular beauty of this "mysticism of every-day life," this discovery of the triune God in everything, this living in the triune God as in our true home. Enclosed in the most tender love of our Abba who gives us being, in Jesus our mother who gives us growth, and in the Holy Spirit who brings us to completion, we are "endlessly treasured" in the God closer to us than our own souls.[15]

Parents who deeply love their children delight in caring for them, in being with and enjoying them. But this joy is only a pale shadow of the infinite gladness the triune God takes in us: we are the Trinity's bliss, and if we could realize how tenderly the triune God rejoices to be God for us, no trouble could finally destroy us. Children sleep in their parents' arms even while everything around them is in confusion and chaos. If they awake, they are soothed with the assuring words, "Everything is all right." We, too, are held in the arms of the triune God; regardless of how frightened or anxious we feel, because we are held in these arms, everything is well, and one day we shall see for ourselves "that all shall be well."[16] For we easily believe that God is all-wise and powerful and *can* do everything, but to believe that the triune God is all love and *will* do everything good for us, "*there* we fail."[17]

We are never to despair; even if through weakness we fall "often and grievously," our falling does not and cannot hinder the power of God's love for us. Julian pictures the scars of our sins being turned into precious jewels in heaven, jewels which both proclaim what God's infinite love has done for us and heal the grief and heartache our sins caused us and others on earth. And so the triune God wants us to "forget our sin with regard to our unreasonable depression and our doubtful fears,"[18] and to live bathed in the ocean of love at the heart of God, for at the end "our shame will be turned into honor and joy."[19]

Julian pictures the triune God, "gentle, courteous, and most sweet" greeting us in heaven with more tender familiarity than the human heart could imagine.[20] Inexpressible gratitude will fill our hearts when we see for ourselves the astounding marvel of the transcendent God's intimate love for us from all eternity. In unbounded, eschatological joy we will forever be "familiar and close to God."[21] This wonderful courtesy and familiarity of our Abba, our Lord Jesus, and their Holy Spirit will come fully to us not from outside us, but flowing within us, drawing us into the unending embrace of their love and delight. "Enter into the joy of your Lord (Mt 25:22)." And then the triune God whose love has given us birth and tenderly enclosed us at every second will become our joy and home forever.

But until then, while we journey here on earth together, what meaning does the triune God have for our day-today-lives, for our own problems and the world's pain? To this final question we now turn.

5

The Challenge of Trinitarian Faith
Today: Implications for a
World Transformed

In previous chapters we have reflected on the meaning of our trinitarian faith in light of Jesus' paschal mystery as well as the community's experiences and faith articulations. In this last chapter we come now full circle to our original question: what does the triune God have to do with the most universal and fundamental of our human experiences, with our loneliness, and creativity and beauty, with our longing for friendship and forgiveness and belonging, with our sin and selfishness and indifference to injustice? What does our faith in the Trinity have to do with the human suffering which confronts us on a world-wide scale; with poverty and marginalization and the abuse of our natural resources; with war and the threat of nuclear holocaust; with unjust social and political structures and the suffering caused by human persons exploiting and oppressing other human persons?

Three interrelated themes underlie our response in this chapter to these fundamental questions. 1) Our Christian faith in the triune God answers the ultimate human question of who and and why we are, for it *interprets our meaning* as a thirst finally not for possession of things, but for interrelationship with persons. 2) Our trinitarian faith in this way confronts us with a *value system* that contradicts a self-centered way of existing in the world and focuses our gaze on the inestimable worth of communion with every human person, especially the most needy among us. 3) Most important of all, the triune God is *healing for our brokenness* and for the wounds deep within us that prevent us from loving and living in mutual respect and care for one another. The Trinity is in fact the very power for our breakthrough from a self-centered existence to a life of mutuality and self-giving.

In this final chapter we thus consider how our belief in a triune God, far from being simply a pious exercise unrelated to our human life and the problems of our real world, is a radical call to conversion, to the inescapable responsibility of relating in and to the world in an entirely transformed way, that is, with trinitarian vision and values.

A. TRINITARIAN FAITH CALLS US TO COMMUNION AND MUTUALITY

It is true that we live in a world embraced in fact by the triune God, but our Christian faith calls us to live this mystery in a conscious way and to take seriously the implications of our trinitarian existence. Our faith in the Trinity thus makes radical claims on us; it is meant not simply to console us but most significantly to transform the way we live. And so we need to ask what relevance the triune God has for our human meaning and for the deepest of our human experiences, especially in how we are to respond to the suffering that confronts us on a world-wide scale.

As we have seen, God's triuneness means that the very secret and heart of our universe is the mystery of interrelational love. And because this is so, we who have come from the hands of the triune God cannot find joy or fulfillment except in living this love in fact. Every sin of our personal lives and of our world, every wound in our individual and social fiber, is reducible finally to our failure to acknowledge and live the love and mutual self-giving which are the triune mystery of our own identity.

Our Christian faith itself calls us to allow the saving trinitarian power in us to become transparent to the world in how we relate to God, to ourselves, to our families, to the earth, to one another, to the most neglected and abused and exploited among us. If we consciously live our belief in the triune God we cannot escape the responsibility of working for families made new by intimate, faithful, and fruitful love. Nor can we evade the task of laboring for a Church reformed in the Holy Spirit, where men and women worship the living God and relate to one another in equality and mutuality; of working for a world in which peace and justice reign, a world peopled by brothers and sisters who inhabit the earth as one human family. Our belief in a triune God thus is no easy, esoteric, merely "spiritual" exercise but a radical way of life. To take seriously the implications of our trinitarian faith means in this way a process of deliverance from patterns of self-centeredness, isolation, and exploitation, and a conversion to habits of relating in mutuality and interpersonal love.

B. THE TRIUNE GOD FREEING US FOR PERSONAL AUTONOMY

The church and world will be transformed when we ourselves are converted by our trinitarian faith. Yet even as we speak this goal, we realize that our indifference and selfishness in the face of others' suffering often come from the unrecognized pain of our own unmet need for love and personal worth, for inner security and a place to belong. We begin our reflections, therefore, by considering first of all how recognizing the triune God's love for us can change the ways we live a closed, insecure, self-centered existence into an open, secure, other-centered life.

1. The God Who Is With Us

When we speak of "experiencing" the triune God's love in our own lives, we may respond that this "experience" has never been ours. The content of our lives, however, is not limited simply to what is available to our senses, to what we can see, touch, hear, taste, smell. The trinitarian love which embraces us as the very ground of our existence is present and active as the ultimate content of all that we experience. There is, therefore, always the unseen "more" at the heart of every moment and event, whether of joy or sorrow, of success or failure, even of sin. All that happens points in some way to the ultimate mystery of love which embraces us at every second. Far from being an unfathomable mystery added to our human experience, the Trinity in this way is rather its very ground and depth content.[1]

Certain events in our life of their very nature lead us to recognize consciously the presence of this trinitarian love permeating the whole of our existence. We know times of joy and inner contentment, when we feel our life to be lovely and full of sunlight. We know, too, times of tragedy when the whole world seems to disintegrate before our eyes. Experiences like these, of creativity and accomplishment, of birth and death, of failure and rejection, of love and commitment are "disclosure" experiences which can reveal to us the love that we perhaps fail to recognize clearly at other times. Events like these can be the occasion for seeing in a deeper way that our entire life, past, present and future, is embraced by arms that are ultimately gracious, good and loving.

But how can experiences of hurt and rejection, of humiliation and disappointment, of failure and isolation, of selfishness and sin, of violence and abuse, dislose to us that we are loved unconditionally and that in the triune God we have a home and family where we belong? It is true that, here, at the very heart of human suffering, we are brought to the brink of the mystery of human existence. But our Christian faith proclaims that this brink is not a wall which shuts us out from love. Because Jesus freely has entered into our human sin and suffering and made it God's own, our pain does not reveal that God has abandoned us but rather that the triune God is *with* us absolutely and without condition.

The proof that we are loved irrevocably is the very fact that we exist. We are loved with unconditional gift-love not because we are good or needed, but because the triune God has loved us from all eternity, loved us when we did not exist, loved us into existence with a love that not only will not be broken but *cannot* be broken. We ourselves love what already exists and is good. But the triune God loves what is not and by this love makes what is nothing into something infinitely valuable and good. Even more, what God once loves can never become unloved.

Because the Word who is Jesus has entered into the depths of all that could destroy us, into the pit of death itself, the final word in the universe is *love*, unconditional gift-love for each of us. We cannot fall out of the arms of the God who has already entered into the chasm of human suffering and filled it with infinite love. For this reason, we do not have to fear standing alone in the truth of our own personal identity, for we are never alone or unloved, never unappreciated or forgotten, never rejected or cast aside. Even in our sin we are loved with a healing mercy immeasurably greater than our guilt. Regardless of the depth of our sin, or the horror of our experiences, we cannot fall from the arms of the God who loves us.

The mercy of a God whom love has driven to become one of us knows our weakness by exprience and loves us with tenderness even in that hidden place within us where we feel most alone and unloved. This self-emptying of a God vulnerable to our human pain is possible only because our Abba is truly source and goal for us, only because there is a divine Word who has been uttered into history for our sake, only because there is their Spirit of love poured out among us; finally, only because there *is* a God who is *triune*.

2. Security in Our Personal Identity

The love of this triune God is continually creating and sustaining us at every second, for our own creation shares in the unending birth of the Word and breathing forth of the Spirit in God. Thus the Trinity is continually knitting together the body and heart and soul, the unique, irreplaceable identity of each one of us with such care that the psalmist's cry is meant to well up from our own depths: "I thank you, Lord, for I am wonderful" (Ps 139:14).

Yet we often see ourselves in a way that denigrates the truth and beauty of who we are in God's eyes. When we look into the mirror of ourselves, we can respond not with wonder and gratitude but with disappointment and shame. We may fear that an abyss of emptiness lies within us and that its uncovering will confirm our deepest suspicion: "Finally, I am worth nothing." Our affective response to our self-image in this way often figuratively resembles the warning label on poisonous substances.

But the triune God is far different. The Word is the perfectly adequate self-image of the Father; there is no disparity between the Father and the crystal clear Word who is Jesus. And the first divine person's affective response to the divine self-image, far from being self-depreciation, is rather the magnificent response of "oohs, and ahs, and eternal applause!"[2] This eternal applause in the heart of God is the very person of the Holy Spirit.

The triune mystery of mutual delight in one another, therefore, has everything to do with the very meaning of our own humanity, with our inmost call to live in love and care for one another rather than in fear and isolation and domination. We who are made in the image of the infinitely lovely Word are meant to enter into the affective self-response, "the oohs and ahs and eternal applause" at the heart of God, and to let the person of the Holy Spirit take hold of *our* being. We are meant to be filled with the same response of delight not only with God but also with the beauty and marvel of our own being in God.

Because we are the home of the Holy Spirit who is more interior to us than we are to ourselves, we do not have to fear loneliness or rejection. If we enter into the depths of our own being, we will find not an abyss of nothingness but the lavish abundance of God's Spirit of love. This truth is highlighted in a story told of Leonides, martyr and father of the third-century theologians, Origen. Leonides would go to his sleeping child, gently kiss his breast, and worship the Holy Spirit who dwelt within him.[3] This story is in some way ours also; we are, each one of us, the temple of the Holy Spirit and the home of God. The very kingdom of God is within us. So to applaud the triune God is always also to throw in some "oohs and ahs and applause" for the beauty of our own mystery.

As we grow more secure in our own identity, our hearts gradually expand to draw us more deeply into relationship with others. For we grow through gracious break-throughs of openness and vulnerability, when we are not afraid to enter into communion with others. We become uniquely who we are as persons only in relation to a "thou," to God as "Thou" and to one another as "thou." The Spirit at the heart of the triune God thus lures us into the sphere of community, of mutuality, and interdependence, for the identity of the "authentic self with Spirit . . . means overthrowing inauthentic individual life for genuine life in union with all."[4]

C. THE TRIUNE GOD TRANSFORMING OUR FAMILY RELATIONSHIPS

Our family and community life is a first key area where our trinitarian faith is meant to transform the way we relate to one another. We know the pain of divorced persons and "latchkey" children; of spouses and children abused emotionally and physically; of family members who do not speak to or communicate with one another. The problems which wound our society as a whole tear at the fiber of our own lives as well. Our addiction to money, power, and chemicals; our greed for material possessions and unbridled sexual license; our lust for violence and crime and war; our disregard for human life; our oppression and neglect of the poor and helpless; our exploitation of one another and our natural resources—these and a host of other forms of human brokenness often are related in some way to our being deprived of love and respect in the context of family life. It is here, at the heart of the pain and evil surrounding us, that we are meant to live the transforming power and values which our belief in the triune God brings to us.

We know by experience how much we have the need to belong to a family of some kind. But this need is ours because we have come from a God who is not an isolated monad but a tri-personal community of love. The divine persons are unreserved self-giving; they hold back nothing of themselves for themselves. All that the Father, Son, and Spirit are, they pour out on one another without reserve. But through the paschal mystery of Jesus they pour themselves out upon *us* also without reserve.

Like the mother and father whose love involves them right where their children are, not only with the smiles and applause accompanying the first step, but also with the mess of dirty diapers and countless sleepless nights, the triune God comes utterly near to us in the Word's incarnation, even into the depths of our sin. Now there is, in the person of Jesus, a radical and reciprocal self-giving between the triune God and us in our own human flesh. The paschal mystery shows us that finally the triune God is satisfied with nothing less than taking us into the intimacy of the divine life, not as strangers but as members of the very family of God.

We know what it is to feel "out of place" in a context that is home for someone else, but not for us. We may also know the gift of feeling so at home in another's family setting that it really *is home* for us. These experiences hint at what it means to say that the triune God has called us into the trinitarian life not simply as foreigners in a strange land, nor even as welcome visitors, but as true "members of the family." The triune God whose gracious love has given us birth satisfies our need to belong by nothing less than the divine life itself.

Through the human, risen flesh of Jesus we are now in the community of the triune God not simply as visitors around a table, but as intimate family members, made so literally by ties of blood, blood poured out for us and which we now drink around the eucharistic table. Through Jesus, God's own blood courses through our veins, God's own Spirit fills our beings. No matter how alone we may feel, the truth more sure than our own existence is that we belong. We have a family. And a home.

The triune God desires to be so intimate with us, so close to us, that in order to make us "a member of the family" that *is* God, God the Son has become one of us. We are not only brothers and sisters irrevocably bound to one another in the family that is God but also in some way brothers and sisters of the *triune God* through Jesus who is forever one of us. And to meet in the most concrete way possible our basic human need to belong, the triune God encloses our conception, birth, and entire existence in a social context. The family composed of father and mother whose love is creative in their children mirrors in an exquisite way the truly primal community who is our ultimate origin and fulfillment, the family who is the triune God. Even the very composition of our human race, our complementarity as women and men, reflects the magnificent diversity in unity at the heart of the triune God. Our sexuality itself expresses our inherent drawing to communion with one another and thus our origin from the God of trinitarian communion.

This is why whenever we gather together in the power of the risen Lord to celebrate his eucharist, we need to expect the Holy Spirit of love to be poured out increasingly in our midst, healing our wounds, binding us together as families and as communities in the triune God, expanding our hearts to care for one another and our brothers and sisters in need throughout the whole world. In this way the paschal mystery of Jesus increasingly gathers not only all of human history but also all of the human race into the depth and force of its embrace.

The early church writers cried out in praise and gratitude, "God has become one of us that we might become God." But we miss the radical nature of this proclamation unless we see that we live as members of the triune God precisely by allowing this God to transform our own lives with unconditional love. "You are the body of Christ ... If one member suffers, all suffer together; if one member is honored, all rejoice together" (I Cor 12:27, 26). In the paschal mystery of Jesus, his Abba has come irrevocably close to us and has given us the Holy Spirit to love one another and all the world with the same gratuitous gift-love at the heart of the triune God.

To take seriously our trinitarian faith and to live from its wellspring, therefore, is to begin relating to our ourselves and others, to our families and communities in a new way. The goals of independence, pleasure, and material or professional success—often achieved at the cost of selfish neglect or abuse of one another—need rather to serve the values of living in mutual respect and interdependence. Our trinitarian faith calls us to commit ourselves to one another, to choose time for and with one another, to listen and speak with respect to one another. It calls us, further, to transform the way we view and live the meaning of our sexuality. Our trinitarian faith calls us to a conversion from patterns of using human persons as objects or of denigrating the meaning of our own self-bestowal by separating sex from the committed interrelational self-giving at the heart of marriage.

Our belief in a triune God urges spouses to relate to one another in mutual love as equals, with neither's needs or personal or professional growth subordinated to the other's. This same faith calls parents to relate to their children not as possessions either to be spoiled or abused, but rather as young persons who deserve respect as well as loving discipline. Trinitarian belief urges parents to give their children their own presence and companionship rather than simply material possessions, and to commit themselves to the mutual communication owed to those who are truly young persons in their own right, with their own unique calls, gifts, and destinies from the triune God.[5]

It goes without saying that this kind of conversion is impossible to our own resources alone, for we relate in a transformed way in the measure that we draw upon the power for love that the triune God is for us. We therefore need to ask for and consciously claim the strength of our Abba's care for us in our need, Jesus' mercy to us in our brokenness, the Spirit's healing in our aloneness. Theirs is the power of interpersonal communion in which we have been immersed in our baptism, a power of love available to us in the sacraments, especially the eucharist, reconciliation, and matrimony. Many of us learn, perhaps too late, that all of the material prosperity and professional success in the world cannot by themselves give us happiness, especially when we achieve them at the price of damaging or losing our spouse, children, loved ones, those to whom we have committed our lives.

Because we have come from the God of interpersonal love, it is literally not possible for us to gain our human fulfillment as selfish individualists. Eventually we learn that we *need* the context of a loving family or community of some kind if we are to find the peace and joy the triune God has intended for us. Our own sometimes painful experience teaches us that we attain our full potential only when we also include in this goal that of consciously committing our energy and quality time to our families and communities. Here is the "place" where the triune God desires us to find the interpersonal communion and joy for which we are made, the intimate love which is meant to heal the world.

D. THE TRIUNE GOD TRANSFORMING OUR RELATIONSHIPS IN THE CHURCH

Our relationships of mutuality and equality in the family as "domestic church" are meant to be a primal experience of the same reality held out to us in the church community. Perhaps too few of us truly experience church as the concrete community of love which binds us together in mutual respect and interdependence in the risen Lord and in the power of his Holy Spirit. Yet this is what the church is meant to be, a living sacrament for us of the triune God's love and union. "By one Spirit we were all baptized into one body—Jews or Greeks, slaves or free—and all were made to drink of one Spirit" (I Cor 12: 12-13).

To begin to take seriously the implications of our faith in the triune God, as individuals and as a church that is both community and institution, necessarily means coming face to face with our need for radical personal conversion in the ways we relate to one another. Instead of being simply the place where, as isolated individuals, we fulfill our Sunday "obligation," "church" would become for us the living family of brothers and sisters to whom we have committed ourselves in love and mutual support. It would be the community with whom we celebrate the death and resurrection of the Lord, and among whom we experience the healing presence and power of his Holy Spirit. Our sacraments would be true *celebrations* full of worship and praise so joyful that others would be drawn by the love and peace they see in and among us. Our sacramental celebratios would then draw us together in other settings to pray and to share our faith with one another, to help each other deepen our surrender to the triune God, and to grow in self-giving love. The bonds of love among us would lead us in turn to reach out as a believing community to the poor, the oppressed, and marginalized. In this way we would begin to experience the power of the liturgy to convert us, to heal and free us from our bondages, and to make us a living force for transforming the world.

Obviously, this kind of living church is possible only to the extent that we as families and communities share our faith, prayer, and love with one another. Experiencing the triune

God's healing presence and power in our local church thus is meant to feed our family and community life, and our family and community life are meant to nourish our faith and self-giving in and to the church.

Our trinitarian faith has still other implications for us as local churches and as the church universal. In the triune God there is no relationship of dominance or abuse, no hierarchy of importance or power, no division between great and little; there is only equality in the communion of love and self-giving to one another and to the world. Because the church of Jesus was meant to be this living sacrament of the triune God to the world, it is only when we begin to take seriously the radical implications of our faith in the God of trinitarian love that we will begin to be this church in truth. His is the community of disciples among whom no great ones rule over the little, the family where authority is not power exercised over others. "The kings of the Gentiles exercise lordship over them . . . But not so with you; rather let the greatest among you become as the youngest, and the leader as one who serves. . . . I am among you as one who serves" (Lk 22: 25-26).

To be the church of Jesus is no longer to divide ourselves into a privileged gender or group or class. "As many of you as were baptized into Christ have put on Christ. There is neither slave nor free, there is neither male nor female; for you are all one in Christ Jesus" (Gal 3:27-28). Church leaders especially have the crucial service of proclaiming God's word to the community not only with their mouths but also with their lives, particularly in how they encourage and foster the irreplaceable ministry of each of us, whether woman or man. In this way the service of every member is meant to enrich the community.[6] To be the church of Jesus in fact thus means to respect and nurture from our hearts the unique value and gifts of each one of us for building up the body of Christ: "For the body does not consist of one member but of many . . . the eye cannot say to the hand, 'I have no need of you'" (1 Cor 12:14, 21). And just as church leaders have the responsibility of calling forth the gifts and ministry of each member, so, too, each one of us has the responsibility of taking seriously our call to foster the growth of the community through our own service of love.

A further implication of our trinitarian faith follows. It is true that, whether we realize it or not, we cannot escape living and dwelling immersed in the Trinity. But we have to recognize consciously and claim this truth in our lives if we are to be the church of Jesus in *truth*. As the Lord's community, we are called to be a sacrament of healing love to the poor and alienated of the world precisely because we are a sacrament of healing also to the broken and alienated and marginalized among our own members. We are meant to know by experience the joy and strength of our communion with the triune God and with one another, to know that in the Holy Spirit we are, all of us in heaven and on earth, bound so tightly by the bonds of infinite love at the heart of God that nothing, not even death itself, can separate us or divide us into groups set against one another. Wherever we go, we will be not alone and alienated but at home—home in the triune God, home in one another.

Further, the triune God we Christians acknowledge explicitly is the same God intimately present and acting not only in other Christian communions, but also in other religions in ways we can even recognize sometimes as anonymously trinitarian. While we cannot develop this point here, we may say with William Hill that even with the profound differences among us, there are hints in the spiritual traditions of the great religions of experiencing the divine in what Christians explicitly "symbolize as one or another of the three who are the Trinity." At the same time, the emphasis on God as non-personal within religious strains of Buddhism and Hinduism, for example, offers a corrective to western tendencies to anthropomorphize God, and reminds us of the truth that the triune God is *trans*personal, that is, infinitely exceeding all that we would identify in our own experience as personal.[7]

Thus the Holy Spirit who binds us together is at work in the world in many varied ways, filling the universe with truth and love, drawing us out of our pride and isolation into communion especially with other Christian ecclesial bodies. Our commitment to ecumenism thus is not an optional extra but a responsibility absolutely central to our trinitarian faith. As individuals, as local churches, and as the church universal we are called to yearn and pray and work for that unity which Jesus identified as the mark of his church: "That they may be one even as we are one, I in them and you in me, that they may become perfectly one, so that the world may know that you have sent me and have loved them even as you have loved me" (Jn 17:22-23). Our unity in diversity in this way is meant to be a living sign and healing sacrament of the triune God's presence in the world. Finally, the Holy Spirit draws us to dialogue, communion and co-operation also with other religions, so that in a world marked increasingly by atheistic values, we will work together to make clearer God's saving love in the world.

E. A TRINITARIAN VISION AND POWER TO TRANS-FORM THE WORLD

Taking seriously our faith in a triune God of interpersonal love also would have radical implications for our relationship to the world around us. It would mean, first of all, a conversion from valuing things over people. Our trinitarian faith of its very nature impels us to relate to every human person, to the most insignificant or poor, to the most deformed or helpless, to the weakest among us, out of the trinitarian vision and values of interrelational love and mutuality. For even with all of the good we are and do, we also live selfishly. In many blatant and subtle ways, we neglect and abuse, we manipulate and use one another in order to look out for ourselves. At the core of almost every other personal and social suffering in our world is our propensity to live in ways that wound or break-up the intimate family relationships which were meant to nurture our mutual love. We value power over people; we nurture and tolerate the threat of nuclear holocaust. We use other persons, especially the most vulnerable and helpless, as means to our own ends. A minority of us hoard the world's resources, leaving the rest of the human race to live and die in abject poverty.

The force of these self-centered impulses within us are evidence enough that the power to love one another and the oppressed throughout the world cannot come from only our own resources. We need the Holy Spirit, the heart of the triune God within us, to take possession of our life through love. The inner security which would come from experiencing ourselves as a treasured and indispensable person in a family and church of equals would in turn help foster in us a growing surrender to the Holy Spirit's love. And it is this love alone which can enlarge our hearts until they know a communion with the entire universe, especially the poorest and weakest of the world.

When we do live this communion with the poor, we live out in fact the implications of our trinitarian faith. This is why our Christian belief in the triune God cannot be separated from our commitment to labor for peace and justice in the world. Yet to transform any situation or structure—familial, social, ecclesiastical, or political—demands from us the courage to relate in mutuality and interdependence rather than through domination of one another. The Holy Spirit is the Spirit of Jesus, who is truth itself. Where there are people who live in this Spirit, people who have the courage to live and speak and relate out of trinitarian vision and values, there is power to transform the world.

This same Holy Spirit, giver of life at the heart of the triune God, labors within and among us to make the universe new through love. Wherever we are committed to sharing in the lot of the poor, to changing unjust economic and political structures in a transformation based on respect and mutuality; wherever we are committed to building a world and church where people are free, where women and men relate to and serve one another as equals, we take seriously the meaning of our belief in the triune God. Wherever we learn to respect and nurture the beauty of the earth, to live in the kind of respect and mutual interdependence that nature itself teaches us; wherever we try to transform through love even the smallest corner of the world, we live out in fact the implications of our trinitarian faith.[8]

For wherever any person suffers, Jesus himself suffers. "I was hungry and you gave me no food, I was thirsty and you gave me no drink . . . naked and you did not clothe me . . . as you did it not to one of the least of these, you did it not to me" (Mt 15:42, 43, 45). And wherever anyone labors to heal and free the world, Jesus labors: "In my flesh I complete what is lacking in Christ's afflictions" (Col 1; 24). And in all of our efforts of love the Holy Spirit works in and among us to unite our world called to manifest its trinitarian origin and destiny through interpersonal love.

F. THE TRIUNE GOD AND CREATING A FUTURE TOGETHER

This love is always a mysterious breakthrough into the future, to a whole new hope and promise for what can be, since love of its nature is a self-transcendence which breaks through the boundaries limiting us to this present moment. When we risk committing ourselves to others, we cannot know what the future holds out to us. But through the communion of love, others' richness becomes in some way ours and our richness becomes theirs; thus, through mutuality and inter-dependence, a whole new future does in fact open to us. When we choose to love and care for one another rather than to dominate one another, we allow the Holy Spirit to open the "horizons of our finite liberty" and to set us on the infinite ocean of the triune God's magnificent, unbounded liberty.[9]

Because we are a people bound together by the unbreakable force of trinitarian love, we do not have to be helpless victims cowering passively before an unknown future. The Spirit of God poured out through Jesus' resurrection lures us together through interpersonal love into a future full of hope. The Spirit of love works within us to heal our wounds, freeing us to serve one another and in this way to choose a future together. "The domain of the Spirit is that of community, of a people's history." The sphere where the Spirit's promptings are felt is "that of a corporate faith and love in which a people, graced with the power of self-determination, give shape to the future."[10] When we are thus converted from seeking power over one another to serving one another, we go beyond the bounds of our own narrow limitedness to *koinonia*, communion.

This cosmic destiny of *koinonia*, of being drawn into the very communion of the triune God, finds a striking portrayal in the Russian icon of the Trinity by Rublev. Three angels, perhaps reminiscent of the three visitors to Abraham (Gen 18:2-8), are pictured as shining youths—symbols of the Trinity—

seated around a banquet table. A continuous circular movement flows through the icon, as the face of each divine person
inclines our gaze to the others. The Holy Spirit is turned
toward the Son, and the Son, through whom we enter the
Trinity, draws our gaze to the Father. The three figures radiate
light and peace; they are seated around the banquet table not
as a self-enclosed circle but facing outward in a posture of
welcome and invitation. They leave a large place open at their
table, a place they have made ready for us as members of their
own family. *Their* table is open to all the world.

A small chalice on the table holds their entire banquet feast.
In the cup is hidden the figure of a lamb, symbol of the
eucharist in which, through Jesus, they feed us with nothing
less than their own *life.* Through this lamb sacrificed for us, a
sacrifice which makes visible the self-giving at the heart of
their own communion, the very life of God now courses in *our*
veins, making us irrevocably their own sisters and brothers as
well as sisters and brothers to one another. Feeding on the
very life of God in the eucharist thus is meant to transform us
into *living* icons of the Trinity, radiant with the self-giving at
the heart of God. Our call is to incarnate in our own lives the
kind of vision which inspired the medieval Russian monk,
St. Sergius of Radonezh. Desiring his monks to relate to one
another with the same mutual love, peace, and communion
that the divine persons are to one another, he consecrated his
monastery in name and in fact to the triune God. Rublev's
icon of the Trinity thus speaks not only of our final destiny but
also of this very same goal for each of us even now: to be as
families, as communities, as church and nations, *living* icons
of the Trinity.[11]

Through us, the whole cosmos in this way becomes a living
doxology to and icon of the triune God. Yet the Spirit not
only is filling the entire universe with the love and presence of
the triune God, but also is drawing us to the eschatological
completion of heaven itself. The Gospel of John pictures us
now like a woman in labor; we cannot escape times when we
weep tears of pain. But the day will come when tears of ecstatic
joy will completely blot out even the faintest memory of pain.
We will look back on our life from the perspective of the
infinite gladness filling us in the triune God and see everything

not as it appeared to be but as it truly was. With the sun bathing us in warmth and radiant light, we will look to where the raging storm used to be and cry out in gratitude to the triune God, "I could not see at that time the immense joy your love would create for me out of sorrow."

Then the paschal mystery in its fullness will be realized in us, the mystery of death which breaks forth into unquenchable life only because there is a God who is tri-personal communion. And the cross which is the "unsurpassable self-definition of God,"[12] proclaiming the infinitely selfless gift-love at the heart of the triune God, in some way will become also *our* self-definition, a mystery of created persons given in unreserved love and mutuality to one another in this same God.

We often know immersion into the cross in our lives now. But we also know in some way the ecstasy of resurrection, of absolutely unexpected gift-love and the break-through of utterly new life. We know the loveliness of song and dance, and the breathtaking beauty of nature; the warmth of loved ones and the brilliance of the sun; the cool breeze on our face and the exhilaration of creating something good and true and beautiful with our science and art, and, even more, with our lives. We know even now what it is to savor the peace of God filling us at unsuspected moments. But *then* our hearts will burst with fullness in an ecstatic gladness that nothing will ever wrest from us.

Then we will know fully, lavishly, what we only glimpse now: that infinite gift-love is the absolute meaning of the universe,[13] that the inexhaustible ocean of the triune God's love and gladness is our beginning and end, our final meaning and goal. We will know fully by experience that the depths of this triune God are the center toward whom all of the universe has been converging, the *omega* toward whom our own life has been inexorably sweeping us. Finally, in this triune God's love and delight, we ourselves and the entire universe will find our extravagant fulfillment and unending home.[14]

Select Bibliography

Augustine. *De Trinitate*. In *Corpus Christianorum Series Latina*, 50. English translation: *The Trinity*. Trans. Stephen McKenna. Washington, D.C.: Catholic University of America Press, 1963.

Bracken, Joseph. "The Holy Trinity as a Community of Divine Persons," *Heythrop Journal* 15 (1974): 166-82; 257-70.

Brown, Raymond. *The Virginal Conception and Bodily Resurrection of Jesus*. New York: Paulist Press, 1973.

Buber, Martin. *I and Thou*. Trans., intro., and notes, Walter Kaufman. New York: Charles Scribner's Sons, 1970.

Congar, Yves, O.P. *I Believe in the Holy Spirit*. 3 vols. Trans. David Smith. New York: Seabury, 1983.

Catherine of Siena. *The Dialogue*. Trans. and intro., Suzanne Noffke. New York: Paulist Press, 1980.

Cousins, Ewart. "The Trinity and World Religions," *Journal of Ecumenical Studies* 7 (1970): 476-98.

de Margerie, Bertrand. *The Christian Trinity in History*. Trans. Edmund J. Fortmann. Still River, Mass.: St. Bede Publ., 1982.

Faricy, Robert. "The Trinitarian Indwelling." *The Thomist* 35 (1971): 369-404.

Ford, Lewis. "Process Trinitarianism," *Journal of the American Academy of Religion* 43 (1975): pp. 199-213.

Fortmann, Edmund J. *The Triune God*. Philadelphia: Westminster Press, 1972.

Guillet, Jacques. *The Consciousness of Jesus.* Trans. Edmond Bonin. New York: Newman Press, 1972.

Hamerton-Kelly, Robert. *God the Father: Theology and Patriarchy in the Teaching of Jesus.* Philadelphia: Fortress, 1979.

Hebblewaite, B. "Perichoresis—Reflections on the Doctrine of the Trinity," *Theology* 80 (1977): 255-61.

Hellwig, Monika K. *Jesus, The Compassion of God.* Wilmington, Delaware: Michael Glazier, 1983.

Hill, Edmund, *The Mystery of the Trinity.* London: Geoffrey Chapman, 1985.

Hill, William J., O.P. *Knowing the Unknown God.* New York: Philosophical Library, 1971.

_____. *The Three-Personed God.* Washington, D.C.: The Catholic University of America, 1982.

Jenson, Robert. *The Triune Identity.* Philadelphia: Fortress Press, 1982.

Jeremias, Joachim. "Abba," in *Abba, Studien zur neutestamentlichen Theologie und Zeitgeschichte.* Göttingen: Vandenhoeck und Ruprect, 1966.

Johnson, Elizabeth A., C.S.J. "The Incomprehensibility of God and the Image of God Male and Female," *Theological Studies* 45 (1984): 441-465.

Julian of Norwich. *Showings.* Trans. and intro., Edmund Colledge, O.S.A. and James Walsh, S.J. New York: Paulist, 1978.

Jüngel, Eberhard. *The Doctrine of the Trinity.* Trans. Hortan Harris. Grand Rapids, Michigan: William B. Eerdmans, 1976.

Kasper, Walter. *The God of Jesus Christ.* Trans. Matthew J. O'Connell. New York: Crossroad, 1986.

_____. *Jesus the Christ.* Trans. V. Green. New York: Paulist, 1976.

Kavanagh, Aidan. *The Shape of Baptism: The Rite of Christian Initiation.* New York: Pueblo, 1978.

Kelly, A. "Trinity and Process: Relevance of the Basic Christian Confession of God," *Theological Studies* 31 (1970): pp. 393-414.

_____. *The Trinity of Love.* Wilmington, Delaware: Michael Glazier, 1989.

Kelly, J. N. D. *Early Christian Creeds.* New York: David McKay, 1950.

La Cugna, Catherine M. "The Relational God; Aquinas and Beyond," *Theological Studies* 46 (1985): 647-663.

Lane, Dermot. *The Reality of Jesus.* New York: Paulist, 1975.

Le Guillou, M.-J. *Le Mystère du Père,* Paris: Fayard, 1973.

Lossky, Vladimir. *The Mystical Theology of the Eastern Church.* Crestwood, New York: St. Vladimir's Seminary Press, 1976.

McCauley, George, S.J. "The Word: Kindly Images," *America,* May 21, 1983.

Moltmann, Jürgen. *The Crucified God.* Trans. R.A. Wilson and John Bowden. New York: Harper and Row, 1977.

Mühlen, Heribert. *Una Mystica Persona: Eine Person in vielen Personen.* Paderborn: F. Schoningh, 1964.

Norris, Richard. *The Christological Controversy.* Philadelphia: Fortress, 1980.

O'Carroll, Michael. *Trinitas: A Theological Encyclopedia of the Holy Trinity.* Wilmington, Delaware: Michael Glazier, 1986.

Pannenberg, Wolfhart. *Jesus, God and Man.* Trans. Lewis L. Wilkins and Duane A. Priebe. Philadelphia: Westminster, 1968.

Pannikar, Raimundo. *The Trinity and the Religious Experience of Man.* New York: Orbis, 1973.

Rahner, Karl, S.J. *Foundations of Christian Faith.* Trans. William V. Dych. New York: Seabury Crossroad, 1978.

—————. *Opportunities for Faith.* Trans. Edward Quinn. New York: Seabury, 1975.

—————. *The Spirit in the Church.* New York: Seabury, 1979.

—————. *The Trinity.* Trans. Joseph Donceel. New York: Seabury Crossroad, 1969.

Ramshaw-Schmidt, Gail. "Naming the Trinity: Orthodoxy and Inclusivity," *Worship* 60 (1986): 491-98.

Raya, Joseph M. *The Face of God: Essays in Byzantine Spirituality.* 2nd ed. McKees Rocks, Pennsylvania: God With Us Publications, 1984.

Ruether, Rosemary Radford. *Sexism and God-Talk: Toward a Feminist Theology.* Boston: Beacon Press, 1983.

Schillebeeckx, Edward, O.P. *Jesus, An Experiment in Christology.* Trans. Hubert Hoskins. New York: Crossroad, 1979.

Schoonenberg, Piet. *The Christ.* Trans. Della Couling. New York: Herder and Herder, 1971.

—————. "Trinity—The Consummated Covenant: Theses on the Doctrine of the Trinitarian God," Trans. Robert C. Ware, *Sciences Religieuses/Studies in Religion* 5 (1975-76): pp. 111-16.

Sheridan, D. "Grounded in the Trinity: Suggestions for a Theology of Relationship to Other Religions," *The Thomist* 50 (1986): 260-278.

Sobrino, Jon. *Christology at the Crossroads.* Trans. John Drury. New York: Orbis, 1978.

Schüssler Fiorenza, Elisabeth. *In Memory of Her: A Feminist Theological Reconstruction of Christian Origins.* New York: Crossroad, 1983.

Thomas Aquinas. *Summa Theologiae.* New York: Blackfriars and McGraw Hill, 1965-1976.

Thompson, William. *The Jesus Debate: A Survey and Synthesis.* New York: Paulist, 1985.

Tennis, Diane. *Is God the Only Reliable Father?* Philadelphia: Westminster, 1985.

van Beeck, Frans Josef. *Christ Proclaimed: Christology as Rhetoric.* New York: Paulist, 1979.

Ware, Kallistos. *The Orthodox Way.* Crestwood, New York: St. Vladimir's Seminary Press, 1979.

Welch, C. *In This Name: The Doctrine of the Trinity in Contemporary Theology.* New York: Charles Scribner's Sons, 1952.

Wilson-Kastner, Patricia. *Faith, Feminism, and the Christ.* Philadelphia: Fortress Press, 1983.

Notes

Notes, Introduction

[1] Karl Rahner, *The Trinity,* trans. Joseph Donceel (New York: Seabury Crossroad, 1969), pp. 10-12.

[2] *The Dialogue* 167; in Catherine of Siena, *The Dialogue,* trans. and intro., Suzanne Noffke (New York: Paulist Press, 1980), p. 364.

Notes, Chapter 1

[1] William J. Hill, O.P., *The Three-Personed God: The Trinity as a Mystery of Salvation* (Washington, D.C.: The Catholic University of America Press, 1982), p. 311.

[2] Martin Buber, *I and Thou,* trans., intro., and notes, Walter Kaufman (New York: Charles Scribner's Sons, 1970).

[3] Karl Rahner, *Opportunities for Faith,* trans. Edward Quinn (New York: Seabury, 1975), pp. 40-41.

[4] *By Little And By Little: The Selected Writings of Dorothy Day,* ed. Robert Ellsburg (New York: Alfred A. Knopf, 1983), p. 213.

[5] Buber, *I and Thou,,* p. 66.

[6] Joachim Jeremias, "Abba," in *Abba, Studien zur neutestamentlichen Theologie und Zeitgeschichte (Göttingen: Vandenhoeck und Ruprect, 1966);* Edward Schillebeeckx, O.P., *Jesus, An Experiment in Christology* (New York: Seabury, 1979).

[7] Robert Hamerton-Kelly, *God the Father: Theology and Patriarchy in the Teaching of Jesus* (Philadelphia: Fortress, 1979).

[8] Diane Tennis, *Is God the Only Reliable Father?* (Philadelphia: Westminster, 1985), pp. 53, 30.

[9] Rosemary Radford Ruether, *Sexism and God-Talk: Toward a Feminist Theology* (Boston: Beacon Press, 1983), pp. 47-71.

[10] Elizabeth A. Johnson, C.S.J., "The Incomprehensibility of God and the Image of God Male and Female," *Theological Studies* 45 (1984), 441-65.

[11] Patricia Wilson-Kastner, *Faith, Feminism, and the Christ* (Philadelphia: Fortress Press, 1983), p. 134.

[12] Julian of Norwich, *Showings,* trans. and intro., Edmund College, O.S.A., and James Walsh, S.J. (New York: Paulist, 1978), p. 301; Catherine of Siena, *The Dialogue,* trans. and intro., Suzanne Noffke, O.P. (New York: Paulist, 1980), p. 292.

Notes, Chapter 2

[1]The insights of this chapter have been strongly influenced by the reflections of Jacques Guillet in *The Consciousness of Jesus,* trans. Edmond Bonin (New York: Newman Press, 1972).

[2]*Ibid.,* pp. 180-82.

[3]*Letter* T 253 to Trincio De' Trinci da Fuligno and Corrado his brother.

[4]Raymond Brown, *The Virginal Conception and Bodily Resurrection of Jesus* (New York: Paulist Press, 1973), pp. 108-110.

Notes, Chapter 3

[1]William J. Hill, *Knowing the Unknown God* (New York: Philosophical Library, 1971), ch. 4.

[2]Robert Jenson, *The Triune Identity* (Philadelphia: Fortress Press, 1982), p. 16.

[3]See Aidan Kavanagh, *The Shape of Baptism: The Rite of Christian Initiation* (New York: Pueblo, 1978).

[4]William J. Hill, O.P., *The Three-Personed God* (Washington, D.C.: The Catholic University of America, 1982), pp. 9, 12.

[5]Jenson, p. 62.

[6]For a study of Chalcedon and the struggles surrounding it, see Richard Norris, *The Christological Controversy* (Philadelphia: Fortress, 1980).

[7]Karl Rahner, *The Trinity,* p. 22.

[8]*Jesus, God and Man,* trans. Lewis L. Wilkins and Duane A. Priebe (Philadelphia: Westminster, 1968), pp. 344; 339-40.

[9]Frans Josef van Beeck in *Christ Proclaimed: Christology as Rhetoric* (New York: Paulist, 1979) analyzes the implications of Chalcedon from the standpoint of the language of proclamation and the intent of that proclamation.

[10]Dermot Lane, *The Reality of Jesus* (New York: Paulist, 1979), pp. 112-16.

[11]Monika K. Hellwig, *Jesus, the Compassion of God* (Wilmington, Delaware: Michael Glazier, Inc., 1983), p. 118.

[12]*Ibid.*

[13]*The Christ,* trans. Della Couling (New York: Herder and Herder, 1971), pp. 85-97.

[14]*Christology at the Crossroads* (New York: Orbis, 1978).

[15]*Sexism and God-Talk,* pp. 54-71; 134-38.

[16]*In Memory of Her: A Feminist Theological Reconstruction of Christian Origins* (New York: Crossroad, 1983), pp. 130-140.

[17]*Jesus the Christ,* trans. V. Green (New York: Paulist, 1976), pp. 245-55.

[18]*Jesus, An Experiment in Christology,* trans. Hubert Hoskins (New York: Crossroad, 1979), pp. 667, 668.

[19]*Ibid.,* pp. 667-69.

[20]*Foundations of Christian Faith,* trans. William V. Dych (New York: Seabury Crossroad, 1978), pp. 298-305.

[21]F. Schleiermacher, *The Christian Faith* (Philadelphia: Fortress, 1976); P. Tillich,

Systematic Theology, 3 vols. (Chicago: U. of Chicago Press, 1951-63), vol. I; C. Richardson, *The Doctrine of the Trinity* (Nashville: Abingdon, 1958).

[22]K. Barth, *Church Dogmatics,* eds., G. Bromiley and T. F. Torrence, 14 vols. (Edinburgh: T. & T. Clark, 1936-69), Vol. I; K. Rahner, *The Trinity,* pp. 109-110.

[23]*The Trinity,* pp. 94-99.

[24]For example, Alfred North Whitehead, *Process and Reality* (New York: Harper Torchbook, 1960).

[25]*The Christ,* pp. 85-86.

[26]*The Crucified God,* trans. R. A. Wilson and John Bowden (New York: Harper and Row, 1977), p. 299.

[27]*Sexism and God-Talk,* pp. 54-71; 116-138.

[28]*In Memory of Her,* pp. 118-159.

[29]*The Jesus Debate: A Survey and Synthesis* (New York: Paulist, 1985), p. 382.

[30]*Showings,* ch. 60; Colledge and Walsh, p. 298.

[31]*The Dialogue,* ch. 141; Noffke, p. 292.

[32]Quoted by Kristen J. Ingram in "The Goddess: Can We Bring Her into Church?" *Spirituality Today* 39 (1987): 50.

[33]Thompson, *The Jesus Debate,* pp. 396-98.

[34]"The Holy Trinity as a Community of Divine Persons," *Heythrop Journal* 15 (1974): 166-82; 257-70.

[35]*The Doctrine of the Trinity,* trans Hortan Harris (Grand Rapids, Michigan: William B. Eerdmans, 1976).

[36]*Una Mystica Persona: Eine Person In vielen Personen* (Paderborn: F. Schoningh, 1964).

[37]*The Three-Personed God,* pp. 262-74.

[38]*Jesus the Christ,* pp. 249-55.

Notes, Chapter 4

[1]Hill, *The Three-Personed God,* pp. 287-296.

[2]Catherine of Siena, *Prayer* 12; in *The Prayers of Catherine of Siena,* trans. Suzanne Noffke, O.P. (New York: Paulist Press, 1983), p. 102.

[3]Julian of Norwich, *Showings,* ch. 61; Colledge and Walsh, p. 301.

[4]*Ibid.,* ch. 60; p. 298; ch. 12, p. 200.

[5]Vladimir Lossky, *The Mystical Theology of the Eastern Church* (Crestwood, New York: St. Vladimir's Seminary Press, 1960), p. 159.

[6]Aquinas, *Summa Theologiae* I, q. 38, a. 2; I, q. 43, a. 3, ad 1.

[7]Walter Kasper, *The God of Jesus Christ,* trans. Matthew J. O'Connell (New York: Crossroad, 1986), p. 226.

[8]*Dialogue* 141; Noffke, p. 292.

[9]Aquinas, *Summa Theologiae* II-II, q. 24, a. 5, ad 3.

[10]Karl Rahner, *The Spirit in the Church* (New York: Seabury, 1979), p. 6.

[11] *Ibid.*, p. 22.

[12] Karl Rahner, *Opportunities for Faith*, trans. Edward Quinn (New York: Seabury, 1975), pp. 40-41.

[13] Yves Congar, *I Believe in the Holy Spirit*, 3 vols., trans. David Smith (New York: Seabury, 1983); II, pp. 70-71.

[14] Aquinas, *Summa Theologiae* II-II, q. 23, a. 2.

[15] Julian of Norwich, *Showings*, ch. 56; Colledge and Walsh, p. 288.

[16] *Ibid.*, ch. 63; p. 305.

[17] *Ibid.*, ch. 73; p. 323.

[18] *Ibid.*

[19] *Ibid.*, ch. 39; p. 245.

[20] *Ibid.*, ch. 74, p. 325.

[21] *Ibid.*

Notes, Chapter 5

[1] Kasper, *The God of Jesus Christ*, p. 85.

[2] George McCauley, S.J., "The Word: Kindly Images," *America*, May 2, 1983.

[3] Eusebius of Caesarea, *Ecclesiastical History* 6, 2, 11.

[4] Hill, *The Three-Personed God*, p. 312.

[5] Cf. Thompson, *The Jesus Debate*, pp. 414-17.

[6] *Ibid.*, pp. 401-05.

[7] Hill, *The Three-Personed God*, p. 309. See also Raimundo Pannikar, *The Trinity and the Religious Experience of Man* (New York: Orbis Books, 1973); Ewert Cousins, "The Trinity and World Religions," *Journal of Ecumenical Studies* 7 (1970): 476-98.

[8] Cf. Hellwig, *Jesus, the Compassion of God*, pp. 121, 153, 158-59.

[9] Hill, *The Three-Personed God*, p. 305.

[10] *Ibid.*, p. 307.

[11] Kallistos Ware, *The Orthodox Way* (Crestwood, New York: St. Vladimir's Press, 1979), p. 49.

[12] Kasper, *The God of Jesus Christ*, p. 194.

[13] *Ibid.*, p. 156.

[14] Hill, *The Three-Personed God*, p. 314.

INDEX OF SUBJECTS